the EDIBLE PEPPER GARDEN

Rosalind Creasy

PERIPLUS

First published in 2000 by
PERIPLUS EDITIONS (HK) LTD.,
with editorial offices at 153 Milk Street,
Boston, Massachusetts 02109 and
5 Little Road #08-01
Singapore 536983.

All photos by Rosalind Creasy, except those that appear courtesy of:
David Cavagnaro: pages 1 *(opposite)*, 43, 47 *(top right)*, 50; Dayna Lane:
pages 38 and 39; Park Seed Company: page 54 *(left)*; Johnny's Selected
Seeds: pages 45 *(above)*, 55, 56 *(left, middle)*, 57 *(left, below)*, 67; Charles
Mann, page 64 *(left)*

Illustrations by Marcy Hawthorne

Library of Congress Cataloging-in-Publication Data
    Creasy, Rosalind.
      The edible pepper garden / by Rosalind Creasy.
          p.   cm.
      ISBN 962-593-296-8 (paper)
      1. Peppers. 2. Cookery (Peppers). I. Title.
    SB351.P4C74 2000
    633.8'4--dc21   99-36394
                                                CIP

Distributed by

USA
Tuttle Publishing
Distribution Center
Airport Industrial Park
364 Innovation Drive
North Clarendon, VT 05759
Tel: (802) 773-8930
Tel: (800) 526-2778

CANADA
Raincoast Books
8680 Cambie Street
Vancouver, Canada V6P 6M9
Tel: (604) 323-7100
Fax: (604) 323-2600

SOUTHEAST ASIA
Berkeley Books Pte. Ltd.
5 Little Road #08-01
Singapore 536983
Tel: (65) 280-3320
Fax: (65) 280-6290

JAPAN
Tuttle Publishing
RK Building, 2nd Floor
2-13-10 Shimo-Meguro
Meguro-Ku
Tokyo, 153, Japan
Tel: (813) 5437-6171
Fax: (813) 5437-0755

First edition
05 04 03 02 01 00
10 9 8 7 6 5 4 3 2 1

Design by Kathryn Sky-Peck

PRINTED IN SINGAPORE

contents

The Edible Pepper Garden *page* 1

All About Peppers 4
The Creasy Pepper Gardens 10
How to Grow Peppers 16

Growing in Your Climate 28
Interview: The Hughes Chili Garden 34
Peppers in Containers 36

The Pepper Garden Encyclopedia *page* 41

From mellow and sweet to hot and spicy

Cooking from the Pepper Garden *page* 67

Marinated Roasted Pimientos 69
Rajas 69
How to Pickle Peppers 70
Pickled Cherry Peppers 70
Sweet Pickled Rainbow Bells 71
How to Make Chipotles 71
Smoky Chipotle Butter 72
Spicy Chipotle Almonds 72
How to Make Chili Powders 73
Paprika Breadsticks 73
Mellow-Yellow Mayonaise 73
Tex-Mex Hot Barbecue Rub 74
Blazo Vinegar 74
Salsa Fresca 75
Salsa Cruda 75
Interview: Doug Kauffman 76
Cherry Pepper Shooters 78
Pepper Ribbon Cheesecake 78
Deep-Fried Squash Blossoms with Chili Cream 80
Walnut-Paprika Dip with Vegetables 81
Watermelon Spicy Salad 82
Fennel Salad with Red Peppers 82
Cream of Roasted Pimiento Soup 83
Cauliflower with Red Pepper Soubise Sauce 84

Mashed Potatoes with Chipotle Butter 84
Peperonata 85
Your Choice Stuffed Peppers 86
Cooking the Dish Chili 87
Broken Arrow Ranch Chili 87
Black Bean and Chicken Chili 87
Garden Chili 88
Babyback Ribs with Ancho Chilies 88
Classic Gumbo 89
Roasted Pepper Garden Lasagna 90
Golden Chicken Curry with Garam Masala 91

Appendices *page* 92

*Appendix A: Planting and
    Maintenance 92*
*Appendix B: Pest and Disease
    Control 97*
Resources 102
Acknowledgments 105

the edible
pepper
garden

As I approached the fairgrounds, I asked myself how I was possibly going to eat all that chili and not burn up. This was my first chili cook-off, and I was a judge. How much chili does a judge eat? Do the folks make it really hot? I like spicy food, but I don't have a mouth made of asbestos like some people I know. I had been to wine and produce tastings, but never a chili tasting. How could I possibly clear my mouth from one bite to the next?

I was early for the judging because I wanted to talk with the entrants about what they put in their chilis. As I entered the cook-off area, I was surprised at the festival atmosphere. The

lawn was surrounded by dozens of carnival-type booths, all decked out. A couple of middle-aged ladies were cooking away in a booth labeled The Hot Flashes. On the sign for another booth was a giant can of Hormel chili with the international prohibited symbol across it—the Hormel Busters, of course. There were the Heart Burners, Chili's Angels, Rattlesnake Rick's, Earthquake Chili, and even a group dressed in camouflage garb proclaim-

ing their chili Rambo Red. Hundreds of visitors were wandering around getting pointers, tasting the chilies, and buying drinks and mouth-watering bowls of chili. What fun!

When it came time to judge the chili, I joined twenty or so other judges in a hall. There, the officials explained the procedure. Cups of chili were laid out on a long table with only a number to identify each one. Between all the cups were trays of soda crackers and cut-up pieces of celery. (So that's how you clear your palate, I thought.) There were also a few bowls of sour cream, used to put out the fire if a chili was too hot. And, of course, there was beer. For guidelines, we were told to ask ourselves first if we would want to eat a whole bowl of this chili. We were to look for depth of flavor—a lasting one—and a chili that wasn't too salty and that certainly wasn't sweet. We were to seek a traditional taste. And

Peppers sweet and hot come in all shapes and colors. Here *(opposite)* are two Italian heirloom peppers used as frying peppers. The yellow one is 'Corno di Toro Giallo,' and the red, 'Corno di Toro Rosso.'

Chilis Angels *(above)* offer some of their chili to folks attending a San José cook-off.

This arrangement of peppers to the right was harvested at the Kendall Jackson Winery trial gardens in Santa Rosa, California. It includes over twenty varieties including 'Yellow Cayennes,' 'Hot Cherries,' 'Poblanos,' 'Purple Beauty,' pimentos, and many varieties of jalapeños.

above all, we were not to talk or make faces. The only communication allowed was a warning to our fellow judges if we ran across a "killer chili"—one that was too hot.

It would be nice to say I had such a sophisticated palate that I picked all three winners, but in fact I liked only one of the winning chilies. It amazed me that most of the chilies were fairly mild, that they varied greatly, but that the winners were quite similar and, furthermore, very salty. The winning chilies were dark red-brown, full of flavor, and smooth in texture.

How did this Yankee, who grew up never eating anything spicier than a gingersnap, wind up as a chili judge? Like many other Americans, for years I had ignored chili and chili peppers of all types. But as my tastes changed and I was exposed to more and more hot Mexican and Asian dishes, I gradually started to enjoy spicy foods. I even began making chili using a commercial chili powder. The result was good,

but when my husband brought back separate chili spices from Texas and I started making chili with selected varieties of ground chilies, what a revelation! Chili peppers weren't simply hot; they actually had complex and varying flavors. This appreciation of fresh ground chilies led naturally to the next step: growing and cooking with fresh green and red chilies of many different varieties. A whole new world had opened up.

all about peppers

All peppers, both hot and sweet, are perennials in the genus *Capsicum* and, along with relatives such as tomatoes and potatoes, are in the Solanaceae family. Peppers originated in subtropical areas of South America and were eventually spread, probably by birds, over South and Central America. Over time they were transported by people to the far corners of the earth and quickly assimilated into many cuisines, often substituting for black pepper. Over the centuries, countless varieties of peppers have been bred to meet the tastes of many different cultures.

There are five species of peppers used for food, but the vast majority under cultivation today are *Capsicum annuum*, which includes both sweet and hot types. A few popular exceptions are *C. chinense*, which includes the notoriously hot habañero, and *C. frutescens*, which includes tabasco and some of the Asian hot peppers. There are also several wild species. In fact, chili peppers still grow wild in many areas of the southwestern United States through parts of Central America and are harvested by the native peoples there.

Sweet Peppers

Sweet peppers evolved from wild (hot) peppers and were bred for their vegetable characteristics, not for their heat. The sweet pepper most of us grew up with was the green bell pepper. Never the belle of the produce section, it nevertheless had its fans. All that has changed, however, as in the last two decades peppers have

been transformed. Americans have fallen in love with peppers. Chili peppers receive the most press and are considered the "sexiest" (they even have their own society), but one look at any supermarket produce section reveals many more flashy sweet peppers than chilies. Since we grew up with only green sweet bell peppers, why, suddenly, can we choose from red, orange, brown, ivory, yellow, and even purple ones? What are these colorful peppers, and where did they all come from anyway?

You're going to have to bear with me here because the answer is a bit involved. First, the easy part. The great majority of green peppers are simply unripe peppers that would turn red if allowed to ripen. Most brown, ivory, lavender, and purple ones, too, are just different varieties of bell peppers, are also unripe, and would eventually ripen to red. Now the tricky part. Some yellow and orange peppers begin as green and turn to yellow or orange when ripe; others ripen to red. However, others start out as yellow or orange and keep their original color when ripe.

As to where they came from, for eons the red ones were but a ripening away from your kitchen. Historically, we Americans have been fairly undemanding about vegetables, and when farmers offered only the green, because they were more efficient to produce and ship, we didn't clamor for other colors. In other parts of the world, especially in Eastern Europe and Italy, they've enjoyed red, orange, yellow, and ivory peppers for ages. (As an

For years, Americans were but a ripening away from great red, yellow, and orange bell peppers. Peppers were harvested in their unripe green stage because it was more efficient for farmers. Now we can choose from a rainbow of peppers and they are oh-so-much sweeter and juicier.

[terminology]

A note about terminology. The word chili, *used alone, can refer to the wonderfully tasty and spicy dish made with hot peppers and tomatoes. However, the word* chili *is also used to refer to peppers. The spelling of the word denoting the pepper depends on a number of factors; it may be variously written* chili, chile, *or* chilli, *as in chili peppers, chile peppers, chilies, or chiles. All are correct, as they are common names derived from various locales. For the purposes of this book, I chose to use the terms* chili *and* chilies.

To experience the color shift as they mature, we laid out three different color stages of peppers, from unripe on the left, to ripest on the right. 'Cal Wonder' and 'Gypsy' are in the top row; a purple ornamental, 'Yellow Cayenne,' and 'Early Jalapeño' are in the middle row; and 'Sweet Banana' and 'Golden Bells' are on the bottom.

Blocky bell peppers *(above)* are the most popular sweet peppers in America. Some of the red and yellow bells have been around for many years, but the lilac, white, and orange bells have been bred in the last few decades.

Hot Peppers

The hotness of hot peppers comes primarily from capsaicin, a pungent and irritating phenol. This chemical is located in the chili pepper's placental tissue, which is found in the light-colored veins on the walls of the pepper and around the seeds. Until fairly recently, the average American gardener ignored chili peppers, so our plant breeders and seed people did not give them much attention. Consequently, most of these fiery cousins are less domesticated than the sweet bell pepper.

While there is an expanding collection of selected chilies, and even a few hybrid jalapeños and poblanos, the less-domesticated chilies differ from bell peppers in a number of ways. The less-domesticated ones are often slower to germinate, and some grow more slowly. A few need very warm weather. Others are more disease resistant than most bells. Chili plants are generally taller, more open, and rangier than bells. Some varieties hold their fruits on top of the leaves in a decorative way, but most produce fruits that hang down. Certainly among the most beautiful vegetables, chili pepper fruits can be large or small, and round or elongated. Unripe, they can be green, black, yellow, orange, white, or purple.

aside, Europeans favor elongated sweet pepper varieties over blocky ones.) Some of the new colors, especially the orange, ivory, and lavender ones, are modern hybrids bred to capitalize on the new interest in bell peppers.

Certainly this chameleon aspect of peppers is interesting, but for the cook it has further ramifications. An unripe green or purple bell has a strong pepper taste and is somewhat sour. In contrast, a ripe red pepper has a rich, more complex pepper flavor and a mellow sweetness. Wendy Krupnick, one-time garden manager of Shepherd's Garden Seeds, said it best: "Unripe bell peppers taste like a vegetable; ripe ones taste more like a fruit." And as any nutritionist knows, ripe peppers have more vitamins as well.

Like their bell cousins, they ripen through a range of colors including orange, or even brown, but most become red. Chili peppers range in hotness from mild to scorching.

Whenever I talk with gardeners and chefs about chilies, the conversation eventually turns to their heat. And the question always arises, What makes the same pepper variety fiery hot one time but mild another? Most of us have planted the same variety and had it come up mild one year but quite hot the next. In discussing this inconsistency with seed people, I learned that there can be different reasons for the variation. Most agreed that the main reason was climatic differences. A somewhat mild chili pepper, for example, might get hotter than usual if grown under the stress of hot and dry conditions. A large difference, however, would be very unusual. A jalapeño might be milder one year than another, or milder in a wet climate than a dry one, but it would still be quite hot, and a mild chili such as an ancho will never be extremely hot.

Another factor affecting the hotness of chilies involves different strains, or subtypes, of the same variety. All jalapeños are not created equal. A generic jalapeño from the nursery, or ordered from a seed company, can vary widely depending on which strain is offered. (For a discussion of varieties and why they vary, see page 41 in "The Pepper Garden Encyclopedia.")

Putting aside the above minor variations, what everyone really wants to know is, Which variety is the hottest? A number of tests have been used over

'Large Thick Red Cayenne' (*above*) is one of many types of cayennes and is very hot. Throughout much of the American Southwest, wreaths and ristras of chili peppers (*below*) are hung on doors and from house eaves to signify prosperity.

the years to determine how hot a pepper is, the oldest being the Scoville Organoleptic Test, in use since 1912 (see page 9 for more information on the Scoville test). Recently the Official Chile Heat Scale has become popular, which rates chilies on a 0 to 10 scale

with bell peppers as 0 and habañeros at 10; jalapeños rate 5, cayennes 8, and chiltepíns 9. Craig Dremann has created his own hotness scale, based on his testing, which he includes in his Redwood City Seed catalog to help you choose your peppers.

The aforementioned scales are all based on human perceptions of heat and are all helpful but obviously subjective. More uniform, objective testing has been done at New Mexico State University using a high-performance liquid chromatography (HPLC) machine. Instead of human perceptions, it records the quantifiable amount of numerous capsaicinoids in an individual pepper. While we think of just one chemical as responsible for the heat, in fact, any one hot pepper contains a number of related capsaicinoids, each with its own characteristics. Some sting instantly, while others take time to bite and build slowly. Some affect the tongue, while others burn the back of the mouth. Their flavors differ as well. Some are described as fruity, while others are musky or smoky. The HPLC machine can quantify the chemicals in only one pepper at a time, and because peppers differ from season to season and plant to plant, it really just gives us a ballpark number. Of course, the question still arises, Which is the hottest? According to Dr. Paul Bosland, who has access to this machine, no matter how many chilies he tests, the habañero always tops the scale.

While the question of how hot a pepper might be is fun to discuss, a very hot chili pepper such as the habañero or 'Tepin' can actually burn you. Craig Dremann recommends that if you're going to eat a chili pepper you've never had before, you should taste it very, very carefully. When he tries a new pepper, he bites into it very slightly with his teeth, and then gingerly tastes the top of his teeth to see what is happening. He then proceeds gradually to bite through the skin and then finally into the chili pepper itself. He avoids using his tongue and lips until he knows the pepper is sufficiently mild.

No matter which variety you choose, peppers hot or sweet enliven the meal and are beautiful in the garden. As gardeners, we have a fabulous choice of peppers, and the mightiest chef can only sigh and yearn for such a flavor-filled option. The following sections will make all your chili dreams possible.

A bountiful basket of the colorful pepper harvest.

SCOVILLE HEAT SCALE

Pepper Variety	Scoville Units
Habañero types	100,000–300,000+
Chiltepíns	50,000–100,000
Thai	70,000–80,000
Cayenne, ají, tabasco	30,000–50,000
Serrano, hot cherry	15,000–30,000
Jalapeño, Fresno	5,000–15,000
Ancho, pasilla	1,000–1,500
'NuMex Big Jim,' 'Anaheim'	100–500
Sweet bells, pimientos	0

[Scoville Units]

In 1912, Wilbur Scoville, a pharmacologist, developed a test to determine the capsaicin content of a hot pepper. He dissolved exact amounts of chili peppers in alcohol diluted with sugar water and had a panel of at least five tasters rate the heat. The hotness was recorded in multiples of one hundred Scoville units. While obviously subjective, this rating did give a rough idea of how hot a pepper variety might be. Today, we analyze peppers' heat using more scientific methods, with a high-performance liquid chromatography machine. The machine-produced numbers are then converted to Scoville units.

The chart to the left gives approximate Scoville unit readings for some of the more popular peppers.

the Creasy pepper gardens

My 1990 pepper garden *(above and opposite)* took over the entire front yard and was interplanted with flowers for drying and for beauty. Both were harvested at about the same time and the bouquets were hung from the garage rafters to dry. The peppers were enjoyed fresh of course, but the bulk was either given to a food bank, frozen, or dried in the dehydrator.

I have an unusual vegetable garden—it's smack dab in my suburban front yard. Twenty-five years ago, I was forced to garden "around front." Our backyard was hopelessly filled with large trees—a redwood, pines, and a fruitless mulberry—and between the shade and the root competition, a vegetable plant didn't have a chance. In those days "veggiescaping" was considered verboten, and when I first planted vegetables around front, I felt forced to plant them surreptitiously in a narrow strip along the front lawn—hiding them among tall flowers. Fortunately, I was studying landscape design at the time, and it wasn't long before it occurred to me that my frilly lettuces, ruby chards, most herbs, eggplants, and my pepper plants were every bit as beautiful as many so-called ornamentals and I could grow them in full view. Of course, planting them in long boring rows and covering the plants with old bleach-bottle cloches wouldn't cut it in the front yard, but well-grown vegetables planted in decorative patterns, or interspersed with flowers, I knew would be lovely.

It was in this same time frame that I was developing my concept of edible landscaping, which was later to become a book; thus my front flower border became part of my many design experiments. For a few years, I experimented with background borders of artichokes, chard, tall chili pepper varieties, and beans; middle borders of sweet peppers, eggplants, carrots, and bush peas; and front borders of parsley, strawberries, lettuces, and small ornamental peppers. As the years pro-

gressed, I found I needed more and more space for vegetables; the long narrow beds weren't big enough and they limited my designs. So, every year the beds got larger and were reconfigured and the lawn got smaller. Finally, about fifteen years ago, the genie was completely out of the bottle, the remaining lawn came out, and I appropriated the entire front yard to grow vegetables and herbs to research varieties for my book *Cooking from the Garden.* That year, I trialed 110 varieties of vegetables in the front yard, and both my husband and the neighbors thought the garden quite wondrous. Once convinced I could make a vegetable garden a social success, I have since grown over thirty different theme vegetable and herb gardens in our front yard. (Since I garden in USDA Zone 9, that includes both winter and summer plantings.) One season, I planted a Native American garden, yet another year I chose a salad theme, and so on.

The 1990 Pepper Garden

In the summer of 1990, I decided that while over the years I had planted many pepper varieties, it was time to explore peppers in depth, and I planned a pepper garden in the beds near the driveway where they would get lots of heat. To intersperse color among the pepper plants, I selected many different types of flowers that dry well for bouquets.

In January, I ordered seeds of twenty varieties of peppers, six special dry flowers, and some choice cutting flower varieties, all by mail. Pepper plants take a long time to get sizable enough to plant outside, so I started them in mid-February, about ten weeks before I planned to plant them outside—namely, in early May. This is at least a month earlier than I start my tomatoes and most of my other vegetables and flowers. I started most of the pepper seeds in potting soil in flats, others in quart containers. I planned for a plant each of most of the bells and hot chilies and a half dozen 'Anaheims' and two pimientos so I would have enough peppers to roast. To get the seeds to germinate quickly, I placed them in the oven of my gas stove, which has a pilot light that maintains a temperature of about 80°F when I leave the door ajar. In reading

the germination information on the seed packages of both 'Tepin' and 'Chili D'Arbol,' I noted that instead of sprouting in the usual seven to ten days, they can take from fourteen to twenty-one days; therefore I planted them in their own container.

As soon as the pepper seedlings emerged, the containers were moved onto my kitchen table and under florescent lights. (Two varieties failed to germinate. I assume, because eighteen varieties germinated easily, that the seeds of the ones that didn't were either too old or hadn't been handled properly by the grower or seed company.) After the seedlings produced their first set of true leaves (the leaves that appear after the first seed leaves), I moved each plant into its own four-inch-square container and fertilized

them with quarter-strength fish emulsion. (You're right, the kitchen smelled awful for a day.) A month or so later, I moved them up into one-gallon containers and repeated the fertilizer. By mid-April, the plants were ready to go outside, and I lined the containers up along an east-facing garage wall to get them acclimatized to the sun and nighttime temperatures. I also found a few pepper plants at the nursery that I wanted to try, and added them to my collection, which now numbered twenty-one.

In early May, my crew and I planted out the peppers. After six years as a vegetable garden—one that had been mulched and babied every year—the soil they were to be grown in was already in great shape, filled with organic matter, and the beds and paths

were in place. The peppers were to be planted in three long rows separated by existing brick paths. Flowers—namely, different colors of statice and gomphrenas and tall varieties of zinnias, cosmos, and lavatera—were spotted around. Drip-irrigation lines were already in place along the beds, and the individual strips of laser line were snaked around and among the transplants and held in place with ground staples.

We had a cool but sunny May and early June, and the peppers were off to a slow start. Once the soil finally warmed up in mid-June, we applied a few inches of compost for a mulch, and in the heat most of the peppers finally took off. The peppers that lagged behind were some of the sweet bells. By mid-August, I had plenty of green jalapeños, serranos, and 'Anaheims' and a few 'North Star' and 'Yolo Wonder' green bells to harvest, but it wasn't until mid-September that the bulk of the peppers started to really produce. And produce they did.

I wouldn't say I had a great harvest, but I had all the peppers I could possibly use and then some. Twenty-seven plants produced baskets and baskets of peppers, and the harvest lasted through October. Most of the bells were used in salads, peperonata, on the grill, and in numerous soups and stews. A lot were also shared with friends, family, and the local food bank. The very hot peppers—'Tepin,' 'D'Arbol,' and 'Thai Hot'—produce lots of peppers, and a little goes a long way. Most of these, and all the different paprika peppers, I dried in my dehydrator to be enjoyed as seasoning

Bell peppers, paprikas, and lots of New Mexico types and hot chili varieties filled my harvest baskets from late August to late October.

throughout the year. To keep them safe from the pantry meal moths that I had in abundance (I found out later that there are pheromone traps that control these kitchen pests), I put the whole dried peppers in plastic freezer bags, labeled them, and put them in the freezer. I had planted six 'Anaheim' and two pimientos, and they produced four big grocery-store bags full of peppers over a six-week period. My daughter-in-law Julie and I spent hours every weekend roasting, peeling, and cutting them into strips so that they could be frozen in freezer bags. Although we said at the time that we would probably never use them all, both of us ran out of them by June. (We both got spoiled because all winter long we were able to make a great meal quickly; from roasted pepper soup for Christmas to a lunch of bean burritos; all we needed to do was reach in the freezer.)

As we pulled the plants out in late fall, I analyzed their health and how the individual varieties had performed

and tasted. I came to the conclusion that most of the bell pepper plants looked sparse and didn't produce as they should have (not that we needed any more), and none looked as vigorous as the many chilies. Further, some of their lower leaves were very pale. In my experience, that means not enough nitrogen, and while all the books I'd read said not to feed them heavily, the next time I planned to give them more nitrogen. For grilling, I most liked the flavor of the anchos and pimientos, but I was disappointed in the productivity and flavor of the purple bells—when I served them in their unripe purple stage, they tasted like green bell peppers. The biggest surprise was the flavor of the 'Almapaprika' pepper; it was sweet, hot, and the essence of pepper. This thick-walled, slightly hot pepper was bred in Hungary for eating fresh, and it tastes terrific that way, but I also dried it for the spice paprika. Because of its thick flesh, it had to be cut in thin slices and dried in a dehydrator, and when it was ground it tended to clump, but who cared, what flavor!

The 1998 Pepper Garden

The 1990 pepper garden was so much fun, I decided to grow another, but this time in a whole new space out by the street because the soil in the driveway beds had become contaminated with nematodes (tiny parasitic critters that invade a plant's root system and stunt their growth), to which most peppers are susceptible. The drainage was poor in the beds along the street, so I had

wooden planters built and a commercial soil mix delivered to fill them. Fortunately, a friend was visiting at the time who is a soil-consultant, and when I told him I usually had problems when I imported soil, he offered to test it. (When you purchase soil from garden supply houses, you seldom know the quality because it depends on where the soil was dug and what was mixed into it.) The analysis showed that the new soil was extremely high in sulfur and boron and practically off the chart in potassium. On the good side, the pH was 7.5, and the soil was high in organic matter and nitrogen. You can see that if I'd had no soil test and added a standard balanced fertilizer, I would have added even more potassium and nitrogen,

and my peppers would have been stunted or would not have bloomed because of the excess nitrogen. My soil guru prescribed a specific amount of limestone to lower the potassium and tie up excess boron. We added the amendment and mixed it in and added no other fertilizers.

It was the year of El Niño and that spring we had record-breaking rain—including thirty days of rain in a row for a total of 40 inches—unheard of in our arid climate, which averages 15

My 1998 pepper garden was created in raised beds out at the street and welcomed all who visited. The driveway beds I had used before were planted with marigolds to control a nematode infestation. The rest of the yard was filled with vegetables and herbs.

The raised beds along the street *(above)*, were filled with peppers. The varieties growing in the bed include 'Figaro' pimento, 'Hungarian Wax,' 'Italian Long,' 'Thai Hot,' 'Golden Bell,' and an unnamed yellow ornamental pepper growing in a container. Two easily grown bell peppers, 'Gypsy' and 'Cal Wonder,' *(below)* grow in another bed.

inches a year. Needless to say, it was a bad spring for getting peppers off to a good start, and I lost 90 percent of my seedlings—all but a few 'Golden Cayennes' and 'Figaros.' I had started the peppers in February as usual, and by April they were big enough to be transplanted to one-gallon containers and moved outside. There, they languished for six more weeks in cold wet weather. (Next year, I get a cold frame.) By the time we were able to plant in mid-June, most of the peppers either had succumbed or looked too pathetic to plant! I decided to abandon my pepper project. But then a trip to a few nurseries yielded a surprising number of interesting pepper varieties. Counting a lovely unnamed yellow ornamental pepper that I purchased at midsummer in a florist's shop, I ended up with one plant each of seventeen varieties and two plants each of the cherries, 'Figaros,' and 'Golden Bells.'

There is considerable evidence that marigolds of all types help deter nematodes. And because most varieties of peppers are quite prone to nematodes, we interplanted the peppers with dwarf marigolds to be cautious. (The driveway beds were also planted with twelve different varieties of marigolds.) When we pulled the gardens out in the fall, there was no nematode damage on the pepper roots (nematodes cause knotlike swellings on the roots and generally deform them) and the driveway beds seemed clear as well.

Considering the very late start in planting the peppers and the questionable soil mix, the pepper garden did well. It produced baskets full of peppers, again far more than we could use. The stars this season were the sweet 'Figaro' pimientos; the 'Golden Bells,' which were enormous, sweet, and plentiful; the big, juicy, and flavorful 'Jalapeño Frienza'; and the cherry peppers. The cherries were new to me, and I really enjoyed them pickled and stuffed for "shooters" (see page 78). I missed being able to roast our usual poblanos and 'Anaheims' from seasons past; and we still don't fully appreciate habañero peppers because they're too hot! All things considered, though, the peppers really came through, the harvest was delightful, and it was such a beautiful garden, cars would slow down to check it out. Who says you can't landscape with veggies?

1990 Pepper Garden: Twenty-Three Varieties

Sweet Peppers

'Big Red'
'Chocolate Bell'
'Culinar'

'Golden Summer'
'North Star'
Paprika

Pimiento
'Purple Beauty'

'Sunrise Orange'

'Vidi'
'Yellow Bell'
'Yolo Wonder'

Hot Peppers
'Almapaprika'
'Anaheim'
'Chili D'Arbol'

Jalapeño
'Mexibell'
'New Mexico'
'NuMex Big Jim'

'Paradicsom Alaku Zold Szentesi'
Serrano
'Tepin'

'Thai Hot'

1998 Pepper Garden: Twenty Varieties

Sweet Peppers

'CalWonder'
'Figaro'
'Golden Bell'
'Gypsy'
'Italian Long'
'Orange King'
'Shishitou'
'Sweet Banana'

Hot Peppers

Chiltepín
'Fiesta'
'Golden Cayenne'
Habañero
Jalapeño
'Jalapeño Frienza'
'Red Cherry'

Serrano
'Thai Dragon'
'Thai Hot'

'Variegata'
'Yellow Ornamental'

how to grow peppers

Like every gardener, I must admit I succumb now and then to impulse buying at the nursery. However, like most gardeners who have spent much time growing peppers, I have learned the hard way that my most successful pepper plantings result from planning and doing my homework. So, before I (or you) touch shovel to soil, here are two critical questions that need to be answered:

1. Where is the best place in the yard for my peppers?

2. What are the best pepper varieties for my climate?

When you have the answers to these two questions, you are well on your way to growing a bounty of beautiful peppers.

Planning Your Pepper Garden

Peppers are tender perennial plants, and only a few varieties have the slightest tolerance for frost. Consequently, most gardeners grow them as warm-weather annuals. They need warmth and sunshine and good soil drainage. Find a place in your garden with at least 8 hours of sunlight a day (except in extremely hot areas, where afternoon or some filtered shade is best). Then test the soil to make sure it drains well. Many of the diseases that affect peppers are caused by poor soil drainage because peppers are quite susceptible to root rot. If you think you might have a problem, the section "Preparing New Garden Beds and Adding Soil Amendments" on page 19

gives information on testing your soil for drainage.

Peppers needn't be alone in their perfect spot. You can add them to a vegetable garden, interplant a few peppers among your ornamentals—particularly your summer annual flowers—or design a new garden. In addition, many peppers do wonderfully in containers or in large planter boxes—which may be necessary if your soil drainage is poor or your soil has fungus or nematode problems.

If you become excited enough to plan a fabulously large pepper garden, there are design considerations, including bed size, paths, and maybe even fencing. Once you plan a garden of a few hundred square feet or more, you need to provide paths, and the soil needs to be arranged in beds. Beds are best limited to 5 feet across, which allows the average person to reach into the bed to harvest or pull weeds from both sides. Raised beds of mounded soil (6 to 8 inches high) are great for peppers because they warm up more quickly in the spring than flat beds do, and they drain well too. Paths through any garden should be at least 3 feet across to provide ample room for walking and using a wheelbarrow. Protection is often needed, so consider putting a fence or wall around the garden to give it a strong design and to keep out rabbits, woodchucks, and the resident dog. Especially tall fences, over 8 feet in height, are needed if deer are a problem because they are great jumpers, and once over, they love to nibble pepper plants to a nubbin, even the really spicy ones!

Peppers are substantial plants *(opposite)*, and many, including the New Mexico types and bells, need sturdy supports or they tend to fall over in the wind. A path between rows gives access to the plants for weeding, maintenance, and harvesting.

The number of pepper plants you plan to grow needs thought. Home gardeners don't need a full flat of jalapeños, no matter how good a deal they get at the nursery. Better to put in two or three plants of a few varieties each year until you find those you most enjoy and that grow best in your garden. With many pepper seasons under my belt, I find that to match the way I cook, and with the number of peppers I give away, I need a minimum of three plants each of pimiento and 'Anaheim'-type peppers for roasting; a few plants of yellow, orange, red, and lilac bells for colorful salads and soups; a few Cuban and 'Italian Long' sweet peppers for frying; a few paprika peppers for drying; three or so plants of jalapeños for chipotle and using fresh; and only one plant each of the blazo serrano, chiltepíns, de árbol, and habañero types because a little heat goes a long way in my family.

Selecting Pepper Varieties

When you choose your peppers, consider not only your dinner table, but also your climate, growing season, sun exposure, and local pests and diseases. You can save yourself much grief by growing the varieties proved best for your region. In the "The Pepper Garden Encyclopedia," I have noted, whenever possible, the regions where a variety usually does best and where it may have problems. Check also with your local master gardeners' organization or with the closest university extension service. I realize, of course,

that it is often in a gardener's nature to want to experiment. When you do, it helps to keep good records so that you can repeat your triumphs.

As a general rule, if you are a beginning gardener and looking for sweet peppers with the least problems, choose peppers that produce the small-

er fruits because some of the very large bells need optimum conditions to produce well. Some excellent sweet peppers that have been bred for short seasons, such as 'Gypsy' and 'North Star,' are perfect for beginning gardeners. Gardeners in northern climates and high elevations also need to look for

Jody Main *(above)*, my garden manager, shows off the pepper harvest from our 1998 garden.

ally needed for the pepper to ripen fully.) I always allow leeway because actual days to maturity will vary with the weather. Cool nights, in particular, slow ripening.

Certain types of peppers grow better in particular areas. Some of the wild chiltepíns, for instance, are triggered to bloom when the days get short in early fall, and in a short-summer area you won't get peppers before frost hits. Further, according to pepper gurus Dave DeWitt and Paul Bosland, in *The Pepper Garden*, "...the New Mexican varieties grow well in the Southwest but not that well in the Northwest and Northeast. Bells and Habañeros do not grow as well in the Southwest as they do in other regions." In sections to follow, I address the particular challenges of growing peppers in cooler, short-summer regions as well as very hot ones.

If you are lucky, or if you only want to grow a few red bell pepper plants and a generic jalapeño, say, you may be able to obtain your pepper plants locally as nursery-grown transplants. If, however, you become a certifiable "chili-head," or if you live in a climate that is borderline for peppers, you will need to obtain your plants or seeds by mail order to get a good, much less a great, selection. Fortunately, peppers are quite easy to start from seed. Most seed companies carry a few interesting pepper varieties, but others specialize in peppers and offer a lifetime of choices. See the Resources section, page 102, for numerous recommended seed and plant sources.

peppers that will tolerate cooler temperatures and/or short-summer growing seasons. Gardeners in hot, humid areas require plants that tolerate diseases, heat, and humidity. See pages 31 and 32 for information on growing

peppers under those conditions. Also remember to look at the days-to-maturity numbers and select peppers that will fit into your growing season. (Days to maturity means the number of days it takes a transplant six to eight weeks old to reach a mature green stage. It does not mean from time of seeding. An additional two to six weeks, depending on variety, are usu-

Preparing New Garden Beds and Adding Soil Amendments

Let's assume that you're hooked on peppers, and planting a variety here and there no longer fills the bill. You now want to grow a pepper garden with many different types. How do you proceed? First you choose a very sunny spot and prepare the soil. If you are one of the few gardeners on the planet with a vacant piece of beautifully loamy soil with good drainage, it's a snap. You just mark out the rows, turn under a little compost, form the paths, and plant. If you're like the rest of us mere mortals, however, you have to start from scratch. This means removing a piece of lawn or removing large rocks and weeds. If you're taking up part of a lawn, the sod needs to be removed. If it is a small area, this can be done with a flat spade. Removing large sections, though, warrants renting a sod cutter. If the area is a weed patch, unfortunately, you will need to dig out any perennial weeds, especially perennial grasses. It's a pain, but you really do need to sift and closely examine each shovelful of soil for every little piece of their roots, or they will regrow with a vengeance and crowd out your pepper plants. Once the lawn, rocks, and weeds are out, and when the soil is not too wet, you need to spade over the area. If your garden is large or the soil is very hard to work, you might rent a rototiller. When you put in a garden for the first time, a rototiller can be very helpful. However, research has shown that continued use of tillers, or regularly turning the soil over by

hand, is hard on soil structure and quickly burns up valuable organic matter if done repeatedly.

Now it's time to take note of what type of soil you have and how well it drains. Is it rich in organic matter and fertility? Is it so sandy that water drains too fast? Or is there a hardpan under your garden that prevents roots from penetrating the soil or water from draining? Hardpan is a fairly common problem in areas of heavy clay, especially in many parts of the Southwest with caliche soils—a very alkaline clay. You need answers to such basic questions before you proceed because peppers grow best with as little stress as possible and their roots are prone to root rot in waterlogged soil. If you are unsure how well a particular area in your garden drains, dig a hole there, about 10 inches deep and 10 inches across, and fill it with water. The next day fill it again. If it still has water in it 8 to 10 hours later, you need to find another place in the garden that will drain much faster, amend your soil with a lot of organic matter and mound it up at least 6 to 8 inches above ground level, or grow your peppers in containers. A very sandy soil, which drains too fast, also calls for the addition of copious amounts of organic matter.

Find out, too, what your soil pH is. Nurseries have kits to test your soil's pH. (The most reliable soil tests are done by soil-testing labs. For recommendations, call your local university extension service or ask at the nursery. In addition to giving you the pH, they can also analyze your soil type and

nutrient levels at quite a reasonable price. This will give you a much better idea of the amounts and kinds of nutrients it needs.) Peppers need a pH between 6.0 and 8.0 and grow best between 6.7 and 7.3. An acidic soil below 6.0 ties up phosphorus, potassium, and calcium, making them unavailable to plants; an alkaline soil tends to tie up iron and zinc. As a rule, rainy climates have acidic soil that needs the pH raised, usually by adding lime, and arid climates have fairly neutral or alkaline soil that needs extra organic matter to lower the pH.

Most soils need to be supplemented with organic matter and nutrients. The big-three nutrients are nitrogen (N), phosphorus (P), and potassium (K)— the ones most frequently found in fertilizers. Calcium, magnesium, and sulfur are also important plant nutrients, and all plants need a number of trace minerals for healthy growth, among them iron, zinc, boron, copper, and manganese. Again, a soil test is the best way to see what your soil needs.

For peppers, most soils will benefit from an application of 4 or 5 inches of compost, 1 or 2 inches of well-aged manure, a phosphorus source such as rock phosphate or bone meal, and kelp meal to provide trace minerals and potassium. If you have done a soil test, you will know more precise amounts. (In future years, you will be able to decrease the amount of additives.) If a soil test indicates that your soil is too acidic, it's necessary to "sweeten" your soil with applications of finely ground dolomitic limestone. (Avoid hydrated lime, quick lime, and slake lime.) To

Good advance planning *(left)* makes for a more productive and healthier pepper garden.

determine the amounts of phosphorus source, kelp meal, and lime, follow the directions on the packages. (If you wish to add fresh manure, it's best to add it in the fall because it needs a few months to decompose. In that case, wait until spring to add any additional compost and fertilizers.) Add a few more inches of compost if you live in a hot, humid climate where heat burns the compost at an accelerated rate or if you have very alkaline, very sandy, or very heavy clay soil.

All vegetables need nitrogen for healthy growth. For peppers, how much nitrogen you add is tricky. Peppers grown in a soil overly rich in nitrogen give you lush leafy growth but not much, if any, fruit. On the other hand, with too little nitrogen, the leaves are small and pale, the plants produce few fruits, and those produced are subject to sunscald because the leaves are too small to cover them. According to the majority of gardening books now available, on most soils, aged manure supplies sufficient nitro-

gen to get peppers growing well. I would agree with that advice when it comes to planting small chilies like chiltepíns, serranos, or de árbols. But my experience with most of the big bells and most hybrids, in particular, has shown me that they need ample amounts of nitrogen. I always scratch into my already fairly rich soil, a handful of blood meal around each plant when I transplant them, and my plants produce a lot of large fruit and lush leaves. Since establishing this routine, I've spoken with a lot of seed people and professional growers on the West Coast and they all agree. They all give extra nitrogen to their big bells and hybrids to make sure the peppers get off to a strong start. (Maybe most of the pepper information comes from East Coast growers, and it's different there.) If you have very sandy soil or one unusually low in nitrogen, I would certainly add an organic source of nitrogen such as fish meal, blood meal, or chicken manure when transplanting your peppers.

Once the plants are growing well and the first fruits are set, most growers agree that all peppers need a supplemental fertilizing with nitrogen to assure a continual supply of healthy leaves. (See "Maintaining Your Peppers," on page 24.) Experiment in your own garden and see how much nitrogen your peppers need. If your soil is already a very rich loam or otherwise high in nitrogen, then nitrogen fertilizer may not be needed. All in all, in my experience, I have found peppers to need more nitrogen than their cousins the tomatoes, which are infamous for not fruiting when overfed. The goal is to give your peppers enough nitrogen to have a good covering of healthy green leaves but not so much that you grow pepper "trees" with little or no fruit. For an even more in-depth discussion of the pros and cons of nitrogen for peppers, see "Nutritional Deficiencies" in Appendix B, page 99.

Potassium, and especially phosphorus, fertilizers work best when incorporated into the root zone. When you add them, sprinkle them evenly over the soil and incorporate them thoroughly by turning the soil over with a spade, working them, and any mineral and organic amendments, into the top 6 to 10 inches. Nitrogen fertilizers, on the other hand, quickly leach out of the root zone and into underground water sources. They are best sprinkled over the soil just before or after planting and lightly scratched into the surface.

Once all the amendments have been incorporated, grade and rake the area. You are now ready to form the beds and paths. Because of all the added materials, the beds will now be elevated above the paths—which further helps drainage. Slope the sides of the beds so that loose soil is not easily washed onto the paths. Some gardeners add a brick or wood edging to outline the beds. In addition, some sort of gravel, brick, stone, or mulch is needed on the paths to forestall weed growth and prevent your feet from getting wet and muddy.

Starting from Seed

Peppers need a long growing season— up to 120 days from seed to maturity for some varieties. The seeds must have warm soil in which to germinate, and seedlings need warm temperatures for growth. It is imperative in most regions to start your plants indoors and move them out into the garden only

after the weather has warmed. Starting seeds inside also gives seedlings a safe start away from slugs, birds, and cutworms.

Start your seeds, in clean flats, peat pots, or other containers with drainage holes, eight to ten weeks before you plan to set them out in the garden. You do not want to transplant them before the soil is reliably warm, which is probably May in much of the country but much earlier in warmer areas, such as along the Gulf Coast and low deserts. In my USDA Zone 9 climate, we have no frosts after early March, but it is May before the weather gets consistently warm, so I start most of my peppers in the middle of February, earlier for some of the slow-growing wilder varieties. Folks in the warmest winter climates often start their peppers in January. I seed mine in either the plastic pony packs that I recycle from the nursery, or in compartmentalized Styrofoam containers variously called plugs or speedling trays (available from mail-order garden-supply

houses). Whatever type of container you use, the soil should be 2 to 3 inches deep. Any shallower and it dries out too fast, and any deeper is usually a waste of seed-starting soil and water.

All containers, equipment, and surfaces should be clean. If you have had a history of damping-off, a fungal disease that kills seedlings at the soil line, then disinfect everything as well. Also, if you are a tobacco user, wash your hands well with a strong soap or disinfect them with rubbing alcohol. Tobacco products may harbor tobacco mosaic virus, which can be passed on to your seeds and plants.

Make sure to use a loose, water-retentive soil mix that drains well. Good drainage is important because soil kept too moist can lead to damping-off disease. Resist the temptation to use garden soil. Commercial starting mixes are best since they have been sterilized to remove weed seeds and fungus diseases; however, the quality varies greatly from brand to brand, and I find that most lack enough nitrogen, so I water with a weak solution of fish emulsion when I plant the seeds and again a few weeks later. (Some sources claim that early fertilizing with nitrogen encourages damping-off disease. I have not experienced this, but if you have had this problem, wait until your seedlings are established before fertilizing with a nitrogen fertilizer.)

Renee's Garden seed company offers a mix of three varieties of cayenne peppers—red, yellow, and purple—all in one package *(left)*. She dyes them before packaging so you can tell which seeds will produce what color pepper.

Fill your containers with potting soil and smooth the soil surface. (Some gardeners like to premoisten the soil.) Plant the seeds about ¼ inch deep and 1 inch apart. Pat down the seeds, and water carefully and lightly to settle the seeds in. With a ballpoint pen or permanent marker, write the name of the species or variety and the date of seeding on a plastic or wooden label and place it at the head of each row.

Keep the seedbed moist but not soggy. Water gently with lukewarm water sprinkled from a watering can, or use a turkey baster to apply the water. Some growers like to cover their seeded containers loosely with plastic, in which case the containers do not need to be watered as often, but you must watch them closely and remove the plastic as soon as germination starts. Germination rates tend to be better when seedbeds are watered from above than when the containers are set in water to be absorbed from below. Bottom watering tends to keep the soil too cool.

Pepper seeds usually germinate best when the soil temperature is in the range of 70°F to 80°F. (They can tolerate higher temperatures, from 90°F to 100°F, and may even germinate faster at those temperatures, but the number of seeds that germinate is usually lower.) Putting the seed trays on the top of your refrigerator may help. However, most gardeners have the best results by using heating cables under their seedling trays. These heating systems need a thermostat to control the temperature (some systems include one). These are available from garden-

Seedlings a few weeks old *(above)* have been thinned and fertilized. The peppers are moved into two-inch containers once they develop true leaves *(below)*, and the faster-growing ones are moved up to one gallon pots. At this stage they are almost ready for planting and can "harden off" in the cold frame.

supply houses or can be ordered from many of the suppliers listed in the Resources section. I don't normally use propagation mats, because I get great results by putting my seed trays in my gas oven with the door ajar, where the pilot light keeps the seed-starting soil in the preferred temperature range. This method does not work with the newer gas ranges that do not have a pilot light.

Check your seed containers every day for germination and moisture content. The seeds of some pepper varieties are slow to germinate, and some may need special treatment—especially if you are starting seed from wild plants. If saving seed yourself, make

sure the pods have fully matured before harvesting the seed. If germination rates are still low, or the seeds take longer than two weeks to germinate, you might try soaking the seeds in warm water for 2 or 3 days before planting; or soaking them in a 10% bleach solution for 5 minutes and then rinsing them well.

Once your seeds have germinated, it's imperative that they immediately be given a quality source of light; otherwise, the new seedlings will be spindly and pale. A greenhouse, cold frame, sun porch, or south-facing window with no overhang will suffice, provided the area is warm (about 70°F during the day and 60°F at night), receives plenty of light, and is not drafty. Or you can get very good results by using cool-white fluorescent lights, which are available from home-supply stores or from specialty mail-order houses. The lights are hung just above the plants for maximum light (no farther than 3 or 4 inches away) for 16 hours a day and are raised as the plants get taller.

Fertilize your seedlings weekly with a quarter-strength solution of fish emulsion, and continue to water them gently. Once all your seedlings are up and have two sets of leaves, you can let the surface (about ½ inch) of the soil dry out between waterings. Test with your finger to see how moist the soil is. Overwatering can encourage damping-off.

If you have seeded thickly and have crowded plants, thin out the weaker ones. Thinning is important because crowded seedlings do not have room for sufficient root growth. It's less damaging to do the thinning with small scissors. Cut the little plants out, leaving the remaining seedlings an inch or so apart. Once seedlings have at least two sets of true leaves (the first leaves that sprout from a seed are called seed leaves and usually look different from the later leaves), move the seedlings up to a larger container, such as a 4-inch pot.

Transplanting Your Peppers

Once the peppers you have moved into 4-inch pots are 3 to 4 inches tall and have several sets of leaves—and the weather is warm—transplant them into the garden. Ideally, the peppers should be just at the bud stage and the weather nicely warm. (They should not have open flowers. If they do, pinch the flowers off when transplanting them.) I know from experience that if I get too anxious and set the peppers out too early, when the weather and soil are too cool, the plants just sit there waiting for warm weather, become stressed, and often don't catch up all season. The ideal time to transplant peppers is when all danger of frost is past, nighttime temperatures are reliably in the mid-50°F range, and the soil has warmed up.

If warm weather has not yet settled in and your peppers are ready to be transplanted, move them to larger containers (at least 1-gallon size) while you wait for the weather and soil to warm. Some gardeners with superior growing conditions, in a greenhouse or such,

When transplanting peppers out into the garden, first prepare the soil well by working in lots of organic matter and adding organic fertilizers *(top)*. Make a hole and place the transplant so it will be at soil level *(middle)*. Put in a label, and gently press down around the plant. If you are using drip irrigation, install it at this time *(bottom)*.

deliberately start their seeds early to extend their short growing season, and move their plants up to ever larger pots until weather permits putting them outside.

Young plants started indoors should be "hardened off" before they are planted in the garden. This means placing the containers outside in a sheltered place a few hours a day for a week or two, leaving them a little longer each day to let them get used to the differences in temperature, humidity, and air movement. A cold frame is a good holding area for hardening off seedlings. Turn off the heating cable and open the lid more each day.

Occasionally I buy pepper transplants from local nurseries. Before setting these or home-grown transplants out in the garden, I check to see if a mat of roots has formed at the bottom of the root ball. If it has, I remove it or open it up so the roots won't continue to grow in a tangled mass. I set the plant in the ground at the same height as it was in the container, pat the plant in place gently by hand, and water each plant in well to remove air bubbles. (I never have problems with cutworms that destroy young seedlings by girdling the plant at the base, but if I did, I would place cardboard collars made from paper-towel tubing around the stems to protect them when I planted the peppers.) I space plants so that they won't be crowded once they mature. When peppers, or any vegetables, grow too close together, they become prone to rot diseases and mildew. (On the other hand, gardeners in hot arid or high-altitude areas can benefit from planting peppers closer together because the overlapping foliage protects the fruits on nearby plants from sunburn.)

I plant most pepper varieties about 2 feet apart, in full sun. Small, short ornamental peppers like 'Fiesta,' 'Variegata,' and 'Super Chile' I plant 1 foot apart and in front of larger varieties, and the spreading tall cultivars, like 'Bolivian Rainbow' and wild chiltepíns, I plant 2 ½ feet apart and behind shorter varieties. I water the plants well at this point, sprinkling the soil gently for three or four applications, letting the water be absorbed between waterings. If I'm planting on a very hot day or the transplants have been in a protected greenhouse, I shade them with a shingle, or such, for a week or so, placed on the sunny side of the plants. If the weather turns cool, I place floating row covers over the plants. Once they are planted, I install my irrigation laser or ooze tubing—see "Watering and Irrigation Systems," page 93, for more information—and if the soil is warm I mulch with a few inches of organic matter. I keep the transplants moist but not soggy for the first few weeks.

Most pepper plants benefit from staking, which I do soon after planting. I have found that peppers in general are brittle and their branches break readily. The taller plants with large peppers, in particular, often lean over from their own weight, and their branches are easily broken by wind or the weight of the fruit. To support them I use recycled wooden stakes, but wire cages, or constructed wooden cages, also work. When using a stake and twine on any type of plant, I apply the twine in a loose figure eight, with one half of the eight around the stake and the other around the plant's stem. I try not to bunch the foliage when tying twine around a plant, as this can cause disease due to lack of air around the leaves. I also avoid tying the twine tightly around the stems because that tends to strangle the plant as the stem grows larger. In addition, a plant will be stronger if it is allowed to move some with the wind.

Maintaining Your Peppers— Watering, Fertilizing, Weeding, Mulching

As a rule, peppers need to grow rapidly and with few interruptions in order to produce well with few pest problems. Once the plants are in the ground, monitoring for nutrient deficiencies, drought, and pests can head off problems. It helps to keep the beds weeded because weeds compete for moisture and nutrients. Some pepper experts suggest pinching off the first blossoms on each plant, which is said to encourage the production of more fruit in the long run. Sometimes I do that, other times I don't have the time or can't bear to put off the harvest. I've yet to document the differences.

In normal soil, peppers usually need a supplemental feeding of organic fertilizer soon after the first fruit has set. Apply a balanced organic vegetable fertilizer or an organic nitrogen fertilizer (such as fish meal, fish emulsion, or blood meal) according to the direc-

Once the young pepper is in the ground, water it in gently *(above)*. I usually apply the water at least three times to make sure the whole root ball gets wet. If the soil is insufficiently warm, mulch the plant with a few inches of compost *(below)*. If it's still cool, wait a few weeks. If you have cutworms, place a cardboard collar around the transplants.

tions on the package. Scratch dry fertilizers into the soil around the plants and water in well.

Peppers need regular watering but not too much—most pepper problems

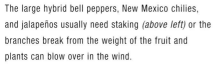

The large hybrid bell peppers, New Mexico chilies, and jalapeños usually need staking *(above left)* or the branches break from the weight of the fruit and plants can blow over in the wind.

Peppers don't need their own garden. Here, 'Golden Bells' were planted in a little garden *(above right)* in the same type of soil and on the same drip lines with zucchinis, popcorn, and tomatoes. A few months later *(below right)* they had all filled in and were doing well.

are caused by overwatering or poor soil drainage. In most cases, a drip-irrigation system is preferable to overhead watering. In extremely hot climates, overhead sprinklers are sometimes used to cool down plants and soil. See Appendix A for more information on watering, drip-irrigation, and weeding.

In warm climates, applying a thick organic mulch can increase your pepper yield as well as save you time, effort, and water. Mulching also helps keep weeds under control. See page 28 for information on maintaining and mulching peppers in cooler climates.

Preventing Pests and Diseases

In most climates, peppers have far fewer pests and diseases than most vegetables. The key to most pepper problems is prevention, which is my emphasis here. If you do develop pest and disease problems, there is information in Appendix B on how to identify and control them.

One of the keys to preventing pepper problems is to understand the role of beneficial organisms in our gardens. Peppers do not grow in a vacuum, and we need to consider the entire ecosystem in which they are grown. This concept was made most clear to me the year the State of California mandated that my county be sprayed with malathion for control of the dreaded medfly (Mediterranean fruit fly). Within a few weeks after the helicopters sprayed our neighborhood, most of my vegetables were infested with insects and my peppers were no exception—they were so covered by aphids and whiteflies that the leaves drooped. I ended up taking out all my vegetables because they were so overrun with pests. Most years I seldom if ever see an aphid or whitefly on my peppers, much less have a problem. That year, nature was completely out of balance, because malathion is a broad-spectrum pesticide and consequently killed off the beneficial insects as well as the pests. Unfortunately, most beneficial insects have a much slower recovery rate than pest insects. Sadly, it was two years before the insect population returned to normal.

When there is a problem growing peppers, a gardener's first thought is usually that there is a pest or disease that needs controlling. Most often, though, different cultural practices are indicated. For instance, if pods are dropping prematurely, it could be due to heat or cool-weather stress, lack of sufficient water, or too much nitrogen fertilizer. Take stock of the conditions and adjust accordingly. Flowers and fruits should return once the situation is corrected. Another condition, called blossom-end rot, which as the name implies produces soft, brown rotted areas on the blossom end of the pods, is not caused by a fungus or bacteria but by a deficiency of calcium.

Sunscald is a common problem with peppers in hot regions with intense sunshine, particularly with the large sweet bells and the New Mexico varieties. It does not seem to be as much of a problem as one might expect for the smaller-podded varieties that display their fruits upright at the top of the plant. Sunscald causes whitish literally cooked spots on the sides of peppers exposed to intense sunlight. If you live in a region where this is a problem, be sure to provide your more susceptible peppers with some afternoon shade to protect them. Also make sure your peppers have sufficient water and nitrogen, so the fruits have good leaf cover. In addition, you might cover them with shade netting or lightweight row covers stretched over hoops with the sides left open for ventilation.

In Appendix B, I have included descriptions and illustrations of some of the common beneficial insects, tips on how to attract them to your garden, and information on blossom-end rot and sunscald.

Two cultural practices that help prevent diseases are crop rotation and soil solarization. For pepper growers, crop rotation means not planting peppers or other Solanaceae family plants such as potatoes, tomatoes, or eggplants in the same plot year after year. Rotating peppers with legumes or other non-Solanaceae plants will deter the buildup of pests and diseases that plague peppers. See "Crop Rotation," page 92, for more information. If your soil already has soil-borne pathogens, such as *Fusarium* spp. or *Verticillium* spp., then soil solarization by the use of clear plastic is probably called for. See "Soil Solarization," page 101.

Peppers and marigolds

Harvesting Your Peppers

Once peppers approach full size, you can pick them at any color stage. For most varieties, though, my advice is to pick a few to use at the green stage but wait for most of them to ripen (change to whatever color that variety is at maturity). They will have much more flavor and nutrition after they have colored up. Hot peppers are hotter, too, if allowed to ripen fully. You will keep the plant producing if you do pick some of the peppers before they ripen, or just as soon as they turn color. Otherwise, plants reach a point at which they stop producing fruit. Selective early harvesting also helps prevent crowding of fruits on branches, which some peppers tend to do, causing the branches to break from the weight. With a little ongoing harvesting, peppers continue to produce fruits until the weather cools, so in the end, it is Mother Nature who has the most influence on the length of the harvest.

Cut, rather than pull, the peppers; if you pull on them, the branches may break. For the very hot peppers, you may need to wear gloves to do harvesting. Both sweet and hot peppers commonly produce from 1 to 2 pounds per plant.

Traditionally, thin-walled chili peppers such as 'Anaheims' and de árbol chilies are strung on string and hung off roofs and porches in parts of the Southwest and Central and South America. This decorative method of drying peppers works well in arid climates, but peppers tend to rot in humid ones. If you, too, want to dry your peppers using this method, the

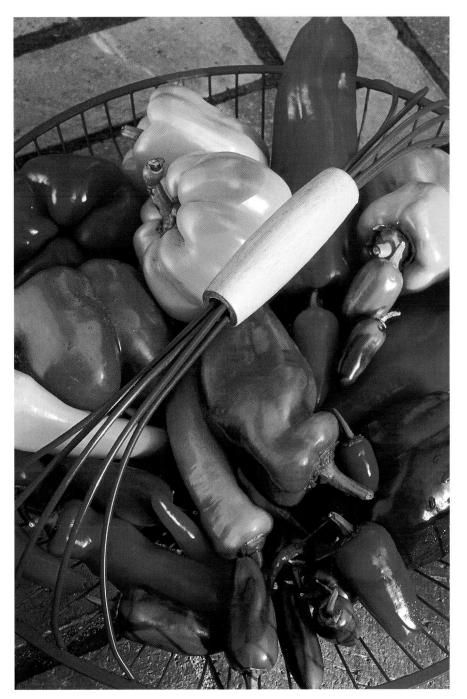

easiest way to string them is to choose a large darning or craft needle and thread it with cotton string that is a few feet, or more, long. Select only fully ripe peppers that have no blemishes or cuts, and push the needle through the stem of each pepper. Leave at least an inch of room between peppers. Hang the string in a warm dry place out of the sun. In a

Fully ripe peppers of all types *(above and opposite)* are your reward for good planning and proper maintenance.

few days, when the peppers are rattle dry, you can move them closer together. For ways to dry peppers in humid climates, see "Cooking from the Pepper Garden," page 67.

growing in your climate

'Italian Long,' 'Red Cherry,' and 'Early Jalapeño' harvested from a Pennsylvania garden *(above)* are all varieties that grow well in short-season cool climates. 'Gypsy' pepper *(opposite)* is one of the few pepper varieties that grows well in most climates, including short-season ones.

Peppers in particular are climate specific. Here, I present the four main growing areas and climates and suggest varieties and techniques that give you the best yield.

Growing Peppers in Northern and High-Altitude Gardens

Few categories of peppers grow equally well in all climates. The problem for gardeners in short or cool-season summers, and often those at high altitudes, is that the short growing season means that slow-maturing varieties fail to ripen or set fruit, and further, some varieties yield poorly. There is some evidence, too, that a few of the less-domesticated chili peppers are not acclimated to northern day lengths and won't bloom until it's too late for fruit to mature. And finally, many chili peppers don't develop their heat under cooler conditions.

How, then, do you get great peppers in cool-summer areas? Probably the best advice I can give is to choose varieties that do well in these conditions, and the best way to find those varieties is through reputable mail-order seed companies. Good catalogs tell you which peppers will or, even more importantly, will not grow well under certain conditions. A few companies offer many varieties of vegetables that thrive in relatively cool, short-summer areas. For instance, Johnny's Selected Seeds, located in Albion, Maine, states in their present catalog that 'Ancho 101' "is best adapted to hot climates, cropping only modestly in Albion." However, 'Thai Dragon' is "extra

early" and fruits are "borne in abundance," and 'Paprika Supreme' is "widely adapted." Johnny's can speak from experience because they trial most of their vegetables in Albion.

Two more seed companies worth seeking out are Nichols Garden Nursery and Territorial Seed Company, both in Oregon. For gardeners in high altitudes, there is also a company in Idaho named, appropriately enough, High Altitude Gardens. All of these companies are listed in Resources, page 102. In addition, I have included regional recommendations, when possible, in "The Pepper Garden Encyclopedia."

To find out more about pepper problems in the north and how to overcome them, I contacted Rob Johnston Jr., owner of Johnny's Selected Seeds; Rose Marie Nichols-McGee, president and owner of Nichols Garden Nursery; and Joel Reiten, research farm manager at Territorial Seed Company. For the Northeast, Rob said that choosing the right variety was critical. He says breeders have tinkered with sweet peppers quite a bit, so there are several varieties available. In the last few years, "Even hot peppers have been substantially improved for growing in longer days, cooler weather, and shorter seasons." He says the key is to look for "earliness." In some varieties, just knowing the days to maturity is not enough. For instance, the anchos, as a rule, do not yield well in the Northeast; yet they do well in the warmer Northwest gardens. In this case it may be the coolness of the Northeast that is the problem.

Some varieties that Rob Johnston particularly likes for the Northeast are 'Italia,' an Italian pepper with "lots of sugar and lots of taste"; 'Big Chili,' an 'Anaheim' that has been adapted for northern gardens; 'Sugarchile,' a sweet-hot pepper with very sweet flesh and hot interior ribs (you can remove the ribs to reduce the heat); and 'Magic Red' for a drying pepper with thin flesh that you can dry without a dehydrator in the humid Northeast (the flesh of most drying peppers is too thick to air-dry in the Northeast).

For the Northwest, Rose Marie says

that while there may be some difference in yield, in her experience most hot peppers actually do pretty well. Even the red and orange habañeros, which tend to set their fruit late, do eventually mature. So she encourages Northwestern gardeners to experiment, try new varieties, and see how they perform. On the other hand, for the sweet peppers, you need to choose more carefully, probably because they have larger fruits, which take longer to mature. For sweet bell peppers, Rose Marie recommends 'Fat 'N Sassy,' which has nice thick walls; 'North

Star'; and 'Jingle Bells,' a mini-bell. She also recommends 'Italian Pepperoncini,' an Italian pickling pepper; 'Pizza Pepper,' a jalapeño type bred for the Northwest; and 'Turino,' a sweet Italian roasting pepper, which Rose Marie says is "lovely."

Joel Reiten also recommends 'Pizza Pepper' for the Northwest. In addition, he likes the Italian heirloom 'Red Bull's Horn,' which he says produces very well, not only in his gardens in Oregon, but in Seattle too. Joel also likes 'Early CalWonder' for a bell that turns red early.

In addition to the above recommendations, as a general rule, if you are looking for sweet peppers, pick peppers with smaller fruits, as they usually ripen sooner than the large, blocky bells. When looking at the days to maturity in seed catalogs and in my recommended varieties lists, select peppers that fit your growing season, remembering that these numbers are averages and that the days are counted from when a pepper is transplanted, not from when it's seeded.

Once pepper varieties are chosen for cool conditions, they need to be started in time to be planted outside when conditions are right, as described in "Starting from Seed" on page 21.

Pepper plants need warmth to get off to a fast start in the spring and for optimum fruit set and ripening. There are three techniques gardeners have found to provide extra heat.

The first is to plant in raised beds 6 to 8 inches high. Mounded soil drains fast and absorbs more sunlight. The easiest way to create the mounds is by

'Super Chili' peppers at the Montreal Botanical Garden are growing well thanks to the extra heat provided by the black plastic mulch.

adding lots of organic matter—it's a rare soil that has too much. Imported garden soil will also work.

A second time-proven technique is to mulch the soil with black plastic, put in place a week or two before transplanting. Among recent advances over the standard black plastic is a green or red plastic called IRT (infrared transmitting) film, available from local garden-supply stores or mail-order garden suppliers. Both Rob Johnston and Joel Reiten recommend the newer, more-advanced materials because they warm the soil more than the black plastic does. As Joel says, in cool gardens, "anything you do to raise the temperature around the plants usually results in a higher percentage of blossoms and blossom set and more color on your peppers." Joel reported that USDA studies are also showing that the SRM-Red film reflects visible light up into the foliage, increasing the rate of photosynthesis, which results in more plant growth.

Black plastic and the newer plastic materials usually come in 4-foot widths. Rob recommends laying the plastic down when the soil is moist—not too wet or dry—and weighing the edges down with soil so that 2 1/2 feet of the plastic is showing. In rainier climates, you probably will not need irrigation under the plastic, but in dryer areas, you need to lay drip irrigation before putting the plastic down. When you plant, Rob recommends using a bulb planter to cut a circle in the plastic. Some gardeners make an **X** with a knife instead. Rob recommends two rows of peppers per 4-foot sheet. In cooler summer areas, this plastic should be left on all season. Don't cover it with any other kind of mulch or you defeat the purpose of the plastic. By the end of the season, the plastic will be tattered, so discard it in the garbage.

The third technique gardeners use to supply needed heat is floating row covers. Cool nights can be a problem for peppers, especially early and late in the season. Joel says that covering your plants with row covers at night, thereby keeping them a few degrees warmer, can make a dramatic difference in the size of the plants and the amount of fruit. For information on row covers, see page 95.

For more information on cool-weather gardening, I recommend *Golden Gate Gardening: The Complete Guide to Year-Round Food Gardening in the San Francisco Bay Area and Coastal California* by Pam Peirce. Despite the title, this book is relevant for cool-summer gardeners nationwide.

There are hundreds of pepper varieties for cool-season gardeners to explore, a great many of which are covered in "The Pepper Garden Encyclopedia." Great variety choices and a few of the heat-building techniques listed above pretty much guarantee a cool-season gardener some dynamite peppers.

Growing Peppers in Hot Climates

Knowing that peppers originally hail from warm climates, one would think pepper gardening would be a breeze for gardeners in hot climates. Not so, say many of these gardeners. When it comes to heat, even peppers can get too much. If the temperature gets too high at midsummer, many peppers won't set fruit, and intense sunlight can cause sunscald (areas that are literally cooked by the heat of the sun) on the fruits. In addition, many regions have special

Sunscald on peppers

others plant their peppers where they will get shade from midafternoon on. As an aside, research has also shown that if you select sweet pepper varieties with small fruits (3 inches or less across), they hold their flowers better during hot spells and therefore fruit better.

Growing Peppers in the Southeast

To learn more about the particular problems of gardeners in the Southeast, I turned to Jeff McCormack, owner of Southern Exposure Seed Exchange in Virginia, a seed company that carries many pepper varieties suited for the South. Jeff says that one of the main problems in the Deep South, though not so much in Virginia, is nematodes in the soil. Nematodes make growing sweet bells especially difficult because many varieties are not resistant to them. Fortunately, two nematode-resistant bell peppers, 'Charleston Belle' and 'Carolina Wonder,' have been developed. 'Carolina Wonder' is also less prone to developing fungus in the seed cavity, another problem that occurs when growing bells in heat and high humidity.

Jeff says that sunscald is definitely a problem throughout the South. To protect the fruits, pepper plants need to have sufficient foliage cover. Jeff says to read the catalog descriptions carefully, select for varieties with good leaf coverage, and keep them growing well.

In addition, Jeff says, southern gardeners must select varieties with resis-

problems such as nematodes or particularly difficult soils.

The good news is that with the right varieties and growing techniques, these gardeners can often get two crops a year from their pepper plants. To do this, however, they need pepper varieties that mature early. Further, plants must be transplanted into the garden as soon as the soil is warm enough in early spring and be producing well before the weather gets too hot. In midsum-

mer, after the first crop has matured, the plants are cut way back to encourage regrowth and then fertilized with a balanced organic fertilizer and kept well watered. Another crop of peppers should follow in the fall.

To help the plants cope with heat, hot-weather gardeners need to mulch their peppers with a thick organic mulch to keep the roots cool as well as conserve moisture. Some gardeners use thick layers of black-and-white newspapers; others use white row covers over hoops to shade their plants, leaving the sides open for ventilation; yet tance or tolerance for the diseases in their area. For a book with a very good take on diseases that southern gardeners face, I recommend Barbara Pleasant's *The Gardener's Guide to Plant Diseases: Earth-Safe Remedies.* Barbara gardens in Alabama and is well aware of the plant diseases that challenge southern gardeners.

In addition to the two nematode-resistant bells mentioned, the sweet varieties Jeff recommends for the Southeast are 'Gambo,' a frying pepper that is Jeff's favorite for flavor; 'Super Shepherd,' a pimiento-like Italian pepper with good leaf cover; 'Corona,' a golden-orange bell pepper that is great fresh in salads; and 'Jimmy Nardello's Italian,' an early, heirloom, banana-shaped pepper that does well in the North or South and is ideal for drying or using fresh in salads. Jeff says that 'Jimmy Nardello's Italian' was highly recommended to him by a gardener in Alabama, and "if it will grow in Alabama, it will grow anywhere."

Jeff says, "There are lots of hot pepper choices for the South. Overall in the South, hot peppers do better than the sweets, as they seem to be hardier." Two that he particularly likes are 'Aji Dulce,' an heirloom aromatic spice pepper that has the flavor and aroma of a habañero but only a trace of heat; and 'Chocolate Habañero,' a habañero with good foliage cover and very aromatic chocolate-brown powerful fruits. Both of these varieties need a very long growing season, so he does not recommend them for areas north of Virginia.

For further information on nema-

todes, sunscald, and diseases prevalent in the South, please refer to Appendix B. For more information on floating row covers, see Appendix A.

Growing Peppers in the Southwest

For recommendations on peppers that do well in the Southwest, I turned to Dr. Paul Bosland, professor in the Agronomy and Horticulture Department, New Mexico State University, and I traveled to Texas to see some gardens firsthand (see the sidebar on the Hughes Garden in Texas). Dr. Bosland says they are able to grow many different types of peppers in New Mexico, even the bells; and habañeros can be grown in home gardens, though not commercially. "The only one we've had problems with is the *Capsicum pubescens* 'Rocoto,' as it likes cooler weather." As to his personal favorites, he says, "I get asked this all the time, and I don't have just one pepper that I like; it depends on how I am going to use them." He says 'Joe E. Parker' is really great for rellenos; he also likes 'Bailey Piquin' for spicy dishes, habañeros for Asian dishes, and 'NuMex Mirasol' to dry for chili powder. Enchanted Seeds, a mail-order seed company listed in the Resources section, carries many of the pepper varieties that do especially well in the Southwest.

Over the years, I've spent time in other southwestern gardens, especially in Tucson and Albuquerque, and become aware of a technique that helps desert growers. Instead of raised beds

to help heat the soil, some gardeners use sunken beds. The beds are dug down so they are 6 to 8 inches below grade. This technique conserves moisture and protects the plants from drying winds. However, the soil must be well drained or you risk waterlogging if rains do come. Which brings up

Southwestern harvest

another problem in many areas of the Southwest: caliche, a condition in dry regions where crusted calcium carbonate forms on certain soils, often forming a hardpan that prevents roots and water from penetrating. Gardeners with a hardpan must either break through it with a pick or posthole digger before they plant their peppers, or garden in containers and raised beds.

All in all, if the correct variety is chosen and the plants are given enough water, pepper growing in hot climates is extremely rewarding. And boy can they get spicy!

the Hughes chili garden

As I drove my rental car from San Antonio to Ingram, Texas, I was struck by the beauty of the countryside. My previous experiences in Texas had been in the dusty border towns. But as I started into the hill country, with the soft gray-greens of the junipers and sages offset by the creamy yellows of the soil and sandstone, I had the feeling that nature had been kinder here. Fields of yellow and mahogany Mexican hats waved in the wind, and as a wildflower fan, I was pleased to glimpse clusters of columbine here and there or bobbing heads of black-eyed Susans. No wonder Lady Bird Johnson, with her ranch not too far away, had become so involved with wildflowers; this had to be their intergalactic headquarters.

I was on my way to Mike Hughes' Broken Arrow Ranch. I had met Mike and his wife, Elizabeth, at a cuisine seminar in San Francisco, where they were promoting their wild game business. During the 1930s, exotic axis, fallow, and Sitka deer had been let loose in the hill country of Texas and were now overpopulated to the point that they were crowding out native animals. Authorities estimate that more than 160,000 of these exotic animals now roam the backcountry of Texas. Mike had formed a company to harvest the ani-

mals and sell the venison to restaurants all over the United States. As we talked at the seminar, he mentioned his recently published book on ranch cooking and his venison chili. The chili sounded so good it piqued my interest, even though I had just finished a plate of smoked duck with endive. As we chatted, I asked Mike if he liked to garden and how he felt about growing chilies. As he was enthusiastic about both, I asked him if he would grow a garden for me specifically for this book. He welcomed the idea, adding that his assistant, Perrin Wells, knew a lot about chili growing. They would be a great team.

As I bounced along the dirt road to Mike's ranch and wound through the trees and clearings, a wild turkey scurried down the road ahead of me. Next I startled a family of axis deer. How different this reality was from my world of asphalt and lawns. And when I approached the chili garden, Perrin went to his car, pulled out his short-wave radio, and called Mike to join us. (Only in Texas, I chuckled to myself, with such large properties, would you have to radio to the house from the garden.) The chili garden sat in a field of Mexican hats just past their peak. As we entered the garden, we passed a raccoon trap. This garden had been plagued by one disaster after another. In fact, until the week before I hadn't been sure there would be a chili garden to visit. Late spring rains had been gully-washers that produced local flooding and were immediately followed by searing drought. Then the raccoons moved in on the corn. But here we were, and through loving care the garden had mostly recovered. Mike began the tour with the chili collection—the 'Jalapeño TAM,' serrano, and 'Anaheim' chilies—and went on to show me the bell pepper varieties—'Gypsy,' 'Golden Summer,' 'Burpee's Early Pimento,' 'Sweet Banana,' and 'CalWonder.' Around the peppers were 'Burpee's VF' hybrid and 'Celebrity' tomatoes, pinto beans, cucumbers, elephant garlic, and what was left of the yellow dent corn after the raccoons had feasted.

Mike and Elizabeth Hughes harvest from their pepper garden.

The soil in Mike's garden is loamy sand, though the sand is limestone, not silica. He first had to improve the drainage by digging the soil well and adding ferrous sulfate to acidify the soil. Each year he also adds organic matter and, because the soil is deficient in nitrogen, a nitrogen fertilizer. In Texas, vegetable gardens are started early in the year, so Mike had planted the garden in early March. Tomatoes, peppers, squashes, and beans need to be in and producing well before the weather gets too hot. In July and August, the plants get rangy and withered looking and because of the high temperature will not set fruit. Mike then takes his tomatoes out, but because the peppers are a little more tolerant, he cuts them back to encourage regrowth. Actually, soon after I left, a big old bull knocked the fence over and ate the garden down to a nubbin, but the peppers recovered to produce a healthy fall crop. After the bull incident, Mike put up a stronger fence and planted his usual fall garden of beans, cucumbers, and squash.

In preparation for the cookout that evening, we went back to the garden when the day cooled to harvest fresh chilies for the corn bread, as well as tomatoes, sweet peppers, and cucumbers for the salad. Texas-style venison chili, corn bread with fresh jalapeño peppers, and tomatoes from the garden—what a feast!

The next morning, as I left the ranch house for the car, an armadillo hopped across the path (I didn't know armadillos could hop), and a bright red cardinal whistled past me. Still remembering the taste of Mike's chili from the night before, I was taking a small part of Texas with me.

peppers in containers

A 'Thai' pepper *(above)* grown as a standard, works well in an old rusty bucket.
Chili peppers of all types are showy in all sorts of containers *(opposite)*, especially blue ones whose colors contrast with the fruits. On the opposite page two unnamed ornamental peppers and a chiltepín I wintered over grow on my front patio.

I plant many peppers in my garden, but I also enjoy growing them in containers. Peppers on the patio are oh-so-handy to the kitchen and, further, using peppers in containers gives me a range of design options. I liken it to hanging pictures in a room—spotting containers around my garden adds interest. If I feel like bright primary colors (which I often do), I bring out my enamel containers, which contrast stunningly with peppers; if I want a cottage-garden effect, I use my aged terra-cotta favorites.

Growing peppers in containers is also valuable for gardeners with small yards, those with only balconies or patios on which to garden, and those whose soil is infested with nematodes or root rots. In addition, as containers can be brought inside, in areas with short growing seasons container growing may be the only way that peppers can be grown to their—much more delicious—fully ripe stage.

How to Grow Peppers in Containers

After years of trial and error, I've found five secrets for success with peppers in containers:

1. Use only soil mixes formulated for containers. I've found that garden soil compacts so that plant roots don't get the oxygen they need. Garden soil in containers also drains poorly and pulls away from the sides of the container, allowing most of the water to run out. It is also often filled with weed seeds.

2. Since containers must have drainage holes in the bottom to prevent the plant from drowning, at planting time I cover the holes with a piece of window screening or small square of weed cloth to keep dirt in and slugs out. (New evidence indicates that gravel or pottery shards in the bottom actually interfere with drainage.)

3. I now use only large containers that provide generously for the plant's root system and hold enough soil to avoid constant watering. Some of the smaller pepper plants will grow in 12-inch containers, but most grow best in containers 18 inches, or more, in diameter. My southern friends report that in their climate, large containers are mandatory because the roots on the south side of small pots bake in the hot sun.

4. Like most plants, peppers in containers need to be fertilized more frequently than those in the ground. Following the recommendations on the package, I mix an organic granulated fish fertilizer formulated for tomatoes into the potting soil before transplanting my pepper plant into the container. I then side dress with fish emulsion every two weeks. Around midseason, I scratch in another round of the same granulated organic fertilizer and top it off with about $\frac{1}{2}$ inch of fresh potting soil or compost.

5. I find that the most difficult aspect of container growing is to maintain the correct moisture in the soil. First, all gardeners need to learn to water container plants properly. Even in rainy climates, hand watering of containers is usually a necessity because little rain penetrates the umbrella of

'Chevena Chujski' and other varieties grow in containers on Dayna Lane's Baltimore balcony *(above and opposite, below)*.

foliage covering a pot. I find that when I hand water, it is most helpful to water the container twice. The first time premoistens the soil (I think of it as moistening a dry sponge), and the second watering is when I feel as though I am actually watering the soil. In contrast to underwatering is over-

watering. To prevent this, I test the soil-moisture content with my finger before watering.

As a rule, gardeners in humid climates should water peppers in outdoor containers three times a week, and in arid climates, daily. However, frequency of watering is dependent on the weather, and during very hot or windy weather, peppers may need to be watered more frequently. A drip-irrigation system is ideal, especially for

those of us who live in arid climates. After years of parched-looking plants, I finally installed a drip system. What a difference! I use Antelco's emitters, called "shrubblers" (available from plumbing-supply stores or by mail order from The Urban Farmer Store, 2833 Vincente Street, San Francisco, CA 94116), as they are tailored so that each container on the system can have the exact amount of water it needs. My drip system is connected to an automatic timer scheduled to water every night for 5 minutes from spring through fall.

Winter Care of Peppers in Containers

In my climate, I do not usually have to bring container plants inside for the winter. So I asked my friend and past assistant, Dayna Lane, for advice. After years of gardening in California, Dayna moved to the East Coast, and with only a balcony on which to garden, she has gained ample experience at four-season container gardening.

"Like everyone, I'm always busy," she said. "So I don't want to bother with dragging too many plants inside to baby all winter. I have found that peppers, however, take little effort and are the most fun of any indoor plant I've grown. In California, I grew peppers in the garden and, like most gardeners, treated these perennials like annuals. But in Baltimore, around late October, when it's time to execute the triage of balcony gardening—which plant stays outside to brave the cold, which goes in the compost, and which gets to come inside—my lovely pepper plants are often still loaded with green peppers.

"The first year I grew peppers in Baltimore, I started sweet 'Chevena Chujski' peppers from seed obtained from Seed Savers Exchange. I started them late and we had a cool summer, so by late October, few of the peppers had turned red. I washed the plants with water to minimize bringing in any hitchhiking insects, and found a nice sunny spot for the peppers in the house. As soon as I brought the plants inside the warm house, the green peppers started turning a gorgeous, rich red. They looked so festive that at Christmastime I hung ornaments on the branches.

"Given a bright sunny spot and ample water, peppers reward me with rich-tasting red peppers for much of the winter. Without sufficient light, pepper leaves get dull and droopy. The dry interior air necessitates watering every day or two, and I mist them occasionally too. They do great until late winter, when the plants start to show the stress of being inside. I begin giving them light feedings of liquid fish fertilizer in February and continue feeding them about every two weeks. Occasionally I wash down the foliage with water because of aphids.

"In early spring, the peppers begin putting out new growth. When the weather is reliably warm, I cut the peppers back to the new lower growth and put them outside. I then move the peppers up to larger containers and scratch in some granulated fish fertilizer. The pepper plants grow quickly, and because they are already established, they bloom and produce fruits much faster than they did their first year, even giving me two crops of peppers. The second crop is often still green when it is time to bring them inside for winter, and for three years now we have had beautiful red peppers for Christmas!"

Before bringing them in, wash pepper plants down *(below)* to prevent pest problems.

the pepper garden encyclopedia

Botanists and cooks categorize peppers in different ways. In this encyclopedia I have addressed both concerns by first grouping domesticated peppers by their species, which are *Capsicum annuum*, *C. baccatum*, *C. chinense*, *C. frutescens*, and the rarely grown *C. pubescens*. Under each species heading I then cluster similar types of pepper pods by whether they are sweet or spicy, then further by the way they are used in the kitchen.

Over the centuries, the naming of peppers has become a muddle. For instance, the identical dark green wedge-shaped pepper is called either an ancho or a poblano, depending on how and where it is being used. In

most of Mexico, where it evolved, it is called a poblano when it is in its fresh state and an ancho when dried. In the United States, when you order seeds, in most catalogs it's designated an ancho, but when you buy the same pepper fresh in most markets, it's called a *poblano,* except in parts of California, where it might be called a *pasilla.* To further confuse the pepper-name issue, seed companies sometimes get creative with vegetable cultivar names, renaming certain peppers to suit their purposes. Consequently, if

you don't know they are the same, you might order seeds of peppers with different names from different companies and end up with two packets of the very same variety. Wherever possible, I've tried to sort out pepper names so you have an idea of which pepper you are purchasing. Alternative variety names are given in parenthesis after the most commonly used name.

The names of peppers is one issue; how to categorize types of peppers is another. On this subject, most of us look to Dr. Paul Bosland for guidance. Bosland is a professor of agronomy and horticulture at New Mexico State University, director of the Chile Institute, and the coauthor of major books on peppers (see the Bibliography). Dr. Bosland categorizes peppers by pod types, a method that after struggling with pepper categories for years, I now find eminently reasonable.

My crew and I enjoy populating the garden with an occasional scarecrow *(opposite)* and this gentleman was just the festive touch one section of my pepper garden.

A harvest from my 1990 pepper garden.

To categorize peppers, it helps to know that certain standard pod types were developed from wild peppers by native tribes long before Europeans set foot in the Western world; those we are most familiar with include jalapeño, serrano, pasilla, aji, and ancho. Other types, while not nearly so old, have been around long enough to become generic standards as well, including Hungarian bred, Hungarian hot wax, sweet banana, and many different paprikas.

When you purchase seeds and plants of peppers, there are differences implied by the names. For instance, you might purchase a plant at the nursery labeled jalapeño. What you are getting in this case is a generic variety. Its pods will look recognizably like a jalapeño, but you have no idea whether it bears

early or late, what diseases it is resistant to, or how hot it might be. Jalapeños from different seed sources have different characteristics. On the other hand, there are many cultivated varieties of jalapeños available such as 'Paul's Piñata,' 'Early Jalapeno,' and 'Senorita,' and in publications they are usually designated by single quotes around the name. Cultivated varieties designated as such have more predictable characteristics. Therefore, when you plant the 'Paul's Piñata' it will predictably have yellow and red pods, 'Early Jalapeno' will perform better in short seasons, and 'Senorita' will produce unusually large, mild pods.

Plants and seeds for peppers are available from local nurseries, but for a wide selection of varieties, you most likely need to contact a mail-order firm. Stokes Seeds, The Pepper Gal, Tomato Growers Supply Company, and Totally Tomatoes carry the largest

selections of pepper varieties. Other companies such as Native Seeds/SEARCH, Redwood City Seed Company, and J. L. Hudson specialize in offering many unusual ethnic varieties, many of which are heirlooms; Evergreen Y. H. Enterprises specializes in Asian varieties; Johnny's Selected Seeds, High Altitude Gardens, and Territorial Seed Company carry seeds of many peppers for short or cool summers; and Southern Exposure Seed Exchange offers varieties for hot, humid climates. Renee's Garden offers a number of selected pepper samplers, which contain two or three varieties of different and superior peppers, in better nurseries. The Resources section gives information on how to contact the many seed companies.

As a final note: TMV in the variety designation indicates a variety that is resistant to tobacco mosaic virus.

CAPSICUM ANNUUM

WHETHER SWEET OR HOT, THE vast majority of cultivated peppers are in the species *Capsicum annuum. C. annuum* was brought to Europe by Christopher Columbus and spread across the globe. Since it cross-pollinates very readily, untold numbers of varieties have been formed, which are cultivated by both home gardeners and farmers around the world. This family of peppers, as a rule, has white flowers and fairly large green leaves.

SWEET

Blocky Bells

Bell peppers, including the ubiquitous sweet green pepper, are the most commonly used peppers in the United States, though definitely not worldwide. They have been given a great deal of attention by modern breeders, resulting in large, thick-walled, usually blocky-shaped peppers, improved disease resistance, and varieties adaptable to less than perfect conditions. Many of the varieties are hybrids. The plants are considered subcompact and are usually 1 to 2 ¹/₂ feet tall. Today, there are more than a hundred varieties of bell peppers. Bell pepper plants are stocky. The branches of most varieties are quite brittle and, when laden with fruit, are prone to break.

Photographer David Cavagnaro's daughter, Carina, holds some of their Italian 'Quadrato d'Asti Giallo' and 'Quadrato d'Asti Rosso' home grown peppers.

Varieties

'**Ace**': 50 days green, 70 days red, hybrid, very early, small to medium fruits, productive, shows resistance to blossom drop in adverse weather, highly recommended for short-season areas

'**Big Bertha**': 72 days, hybrid, green to red, large bells ideal for stuffing, 7-by-4-inch fruits, thick flesh, 30-inch plants, resistant to TMV, adaptable, successful in Northeast

'**CalWonder**' ('California Wonder'): 75 days, green to red, heirloom, among earliest bell peppers, resistant to TMV and southern blight disease 'Early CalWonder' sets fruit a week earlier and tolerates cooler conditions.

'**Carolina Wonder**': 75 days, green to red, 3 inches square, nematode resistant, developed for southern gardens, resists fungus in seed cavity, carried by Southern Exposure Seed Exchange

'Golden Summer' *(above)*; 'Golden Bell' *(below)*

'Lilac Bell' *(above)*;'Purple Beauty' *(below)*

'Charleston Belle': 67 days, green to red, 3 inches square, nematode resistant, bell pepper developed for southern gardens, carried by Southern Exposure Seed Exchange

'Chocolate Beauty': 70 days to green, 90 days to chocolate color, hybrid, medium-sized fruits, thick, crispy flesh (without a chocolate flavor), resists TMV

'Earlired': 85 days, bell type, ripens to red even in cool, wet summer weather

'Early Crisp': 60 days, medium-size, green to red, reported to produce along Gulf Coast before weather gets too hot

'Fat 'N Sassy': 65 days green, 78 days red; hybrid; big, extra early, glossy red fruits, thick, juicy walls; compact plants; vigorous; high yields; good for the Northwest

'Gator Bell': 75 days, bright green to red, hybid, large, prolific plants, leaves give good sunscald protection, resistant to TMV

'Golden Bell': 72 days, hybrid, large, sweet, juicy, light yellow to golden peppers, vigorous, productive, compact plants, one of the best

'Golden Summer': 70 days, hybrid, large, lime green to yellow-gold, high yields, TMV resistant

'Jingle Bells': 60 days, hybrid, miniature bells, 1 1/2 inch blocky green to red fruits, early, compact plants, prolific, great for containers, TMV tolerant, does well in the Northwest and mid-Atlantic regions

'Ivory': 68 days, hybrid, 4 by 3 1/2 inches, rich ivory white ripening to yellow, medium-sized fruit, TMV resistant

'Lilac': 70 days, hybrid, ivory to lavender to crimson with extended lavender stage, blocky fruits, thick flesh, sweet, vigorous, TMV resistant, better coloring than purple bell

'North Star': 60 days green, 80 days bright red; hybrid; early; medium-large, thick-walled fruits; excellent for short-seasons; sets fruit under adverse conditions; productive; TMV resistant; great for beginners

'Purple Beauty': 70 days, green to deep purple to red, productive, TMV resistant

'Quadrato D'Asti Giallo': 85 days, green to gold Italian pepper, very large, productive, has red equivalent, 'Quadrato D'Asti Rosso'

'Super Greygo II': 68 days, hybrid, large, 6 by 4 ½ inches, red cheese type with thick flesh, good for stuffing, TMV tolerant

'Yankee Bell': 60 days green, 80 days red, medium-sized, thick-walled fruit; developed by Johnny's Selected Seeds for northern gardens

How to prepare: Most Europeans are amazed that Americans eat immature green bell peppers. They consider unripe peppers hard to digest and a bit like eating unripe melons. In substance I agree with them, as ripe bell peppers have oh-so-much more flavor and sweetness. But I do enjoy a green bell occasionally in dishes like a Boston-style steak sandwich and on pizza.

Some bell pepper basics: The riper the pepper, the sweeter, and the more vitamins A, C, and beta-carotene it has. It's not always obvious when a pepper is ripe, as it depends on the variety. Basically, even when they start out another color such as purple or yellow, most varieties of bell peppers turn red or orange (a few turn dark brown) when they are ripe. Catalogs tell gardeners what color a variety is when it is ripe. If the pepper starts to wrinkle, it is overripe. As the pepper ripens, the skin tends to get tougher. If you are using them raw in a recipe and if the skins are a little tough, chop or mince them. If you are using them cooked,

'Yankee Bell' *(top),* 'Super Greygo II' *(bottom)*

roast them and remove the peel, as described on page 68.

I enjoy bells in their red, yellow, and orange stage as staples for summer meals. I add strips or rings raw to salads; use bells stuffed with tuna, chicken, an herb risotto, corn and chilies, or other cold salads; or, for a beautiful

hors d'oeuvre tray, I mix slices of the different-colored varieties and offer flavorful dips. This is a lovely use of the chocolate, lavender, and ivory varieties as it shows off their colors, remembering that they have less flavor and sweetness than fully ripe bells, and if you use them cooked they lose most of their unique color. My favorite way to serve the colorful bell peppers is to grill them and use the meaty peeled strips in soups, winter squash stew, omelets and frittatas, layered in a savory bread pudding, and ground into a paste to use in sandwiches; in spreads with olives, garlic, and anchovies, and as a soubise sauce for cauliflower and fish (see recipe on page 84). Occasionally I pickle them and line up strips of different colors in the jar, as described on page 68.

There are numerous dishes in which green or red bell peppers can shine. They are traditional in gumbos such as the recipe on page 89 and jambalaya, and what would a Cantonese/American stir-fry such as sweet-and-sour pork be without them? In India, bell peppers are occasionally used in curries such as the one on page 91, and in the Middle East bell pepper chunks alternate with lamb or beef on shish kebabs. Many cooks in the Southwest use them in regional cooking, but pepper maven Mark Miller finds bell peppers seldom interchangeable with New Mexico and ancho peppers. To him, they lack complexity of flavor and don't blend well with most Mexican and southwestern seasonings.

Elongated Sweet Peppers

There are a number of similar sweet peppers that can be grouped by pod type. These include Cubanelles (Cubans), elongated European bells, and so-called Italian peppers, and they are all ideal for basic pepper cooking. As a rule, these peppers tend to be longer and more narrow than American bells, and some say they are more flavorful. They usually have thin to medium-thick flesh. Cubanelles are slender and may be from 2 to 10 inches long, red, orange, or yellow, and over the years, while most evolved in Italy, have become associated with Caribbean cooking. European bells are more tapered than the blocky-shaped American bells. Pod color on these peppers ranges from yellowish green when immature, to red or reddish orange when ripe. The plants are between 2 and 3 feet tall. Italian peppers are similar to the Cubanelles, but some have longer, less-pointed pods.

Varieties

'Aruba': 65 days, Cubanelle-type long popular in the Caribbean, lime green to orange to red, thin walled, crisp, juicy, best as a frying pepper, vigorous, prolific, about 2 feet tall

'Biscayne': 70 days, hybrid, light green maturing to reddish orange, Cubanelle-type, fruits 6 $^{1}/_{2}$ inches long, vigorous plants set fruits for several weeks

'Cadice': 55 days, hybrid, green to red, early, very large, blocky, French, vigorous, compact plants adaptable to cool regions, short seasons, containers, available from Shepherd's Garden Seeds

'Corno di Toro Giallo'('Yellow Bull's Horn'): 90 days; yellow at maturity, Italian pepper shaped like a bull's horn, 6 to 12 inches long

'Corno di Toro Rosso' ('Red Bull's Horn'): 90 days, red version of 'Corno di Toro Giallo,' does well in Northwest

'Cubanelle': 65 days, green to yellow to orange or red, 5 by 2 inches

'Gambo': 62 days, green to red, flattened bell, thick flesh, recommended for the South, Jeff McCormack's favorite for flavor, available from Southern Exposure Seed Exchange

'Gypsy': 60 days pale yellow, 78 days orange-red, hybrid, very early, sweet when ripe, thin-walled, to 5 inches long, wedge-shaped, European-type bell, productive, 1981 All-America Selection, performs in hot, cold, and mountain regions, TMV resistant, good for beginners

'Italia': 55 days green, 75 days red, Italian pepper, similar to 'Corno di Toro Rosso,' 8-by-2 $^{1}/_{2}$-inch fruits, early, sweet, full pepper flavor, productive, good for Northwest

'Italian Long Sweet' ('Italian Sweet'): 70 days, bright green to red, 7 by 2 inches, tapering, good for the Northeast

'Jimmy Nardello's Italian': 75 days, green to red, heirloom, banana-shaped pepper, widely adapted

'Mandarin': 75 days, deep pumpkin orange, hybrid, 6-inch-long European bell, distinctive sweet flavor, TMV resistant

Pepperoncini: 75 days, usually harvested when light green and full size, turns red at maturity, slender, to 4 inches long, mild spiciness, very adaptable,

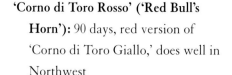

A harvest of 'Biscayne,' 'Cubanelle,' and 'Italian Long Sweet'.

does well in the Northwest, most often used pickled in Italian antipasto

'Snow White': pale yellow European bell with touch of spice, Rose Marie Nichols McGee of Nichols Garden Nursery says this pepper is popular in Bosnia where she saw truckloads of it but new to the United States, delicious for stuffing and baking

'Turino': 55 days green, 75 red, Italian roasting pepper, early, thicker walled than some roasting peppers, use in its ripe red stage

'Vidi': 70 days, green to red, French hybrid, European-style bell, sets well under extreme conditions, compact bush

How to prepare: Cubanelles and the Italian-style peppers are delicious fried, their traditional method of preparation. In the Caribbean, among many uses, the fried peppers are served alongside eggs or chorizo (a spicy sausage), added to stews, and sometimes end up with roast pork in a Cuban sandwich.

Italian peppers are traditionally sliced and fried in olive oil and garlic to accompany meats, eggs, and pasta; or braised with onions and tomatoes and served as a side dish called *peperonata,* for which you will find a recipe on page 85. Sometimes the fried peppers are sliced and served in a baguette with tomatoes and basil. The large peppers are occasionally stuffed with bread crumbs, capers, anchovies, and olives or with a flavored pasta. Italians also roast these sweet peppers and marinate them with garlic and savory

herbs for antipastos. You will find a recipe on page 69. You might also use them in a sauce for pasta along with anchovies or pancetta. In a few parts of southern Italy, these peppers are dried like tomatoes and used over the winter; made into a paste and spread on bread; or used as a condiment.

In eastern Europe, these peppers are often found in combination with a sweet or spicy paprika, as in a paprika gravy, in stuffed cabbage, or in a

Clockwise from top left: 'Red Gypsy,' 'Corno di Toro' and 'Corno di Gallo,' pepperocini, and 'Yellow Gypsy'

Bulgarian spread called *kiopoolu* with roasted eggplants and spices. According to Rose Marie Nichols McGee: In Bosnia, 'Snow White' is cut in half vertically, stuffed with rice, meat, and tomatoes, laid on its side and baked, basted often with tomato sauce.

Paprika/Spice Pepper

Paprika is the Hungarian name for peppers of all types, including those enjoyed as a vegetable and the ones dried and used as a spice. When the fruits are harvested, the thin-walled ones are often strung and hung up to dry under the eaves of the house. The pods are then seeded and ground for paprika powder. Paprika pods range from flattened globes to conical shapes. Pod color ranges from green or pale yellow when immature to dark red when mature.

In Hungary, spice paprikas are bred for their unique flavor and for thin flesh that dries quickly. Even though they are billed as sweet peppers, many actually have a hint of pungency. Their distinctive flavor is essential in Hungarian cooking. Peter Kopcinski, Hungarian pepper authority and owner of Burkop Seeds, a wholesale seed company specializing in peppers, says that these peppers are "… so wonderful, it's hard for me to make a soup without wanting to throw a Hungarian pepper in it."

In addition to using the peppers in soups or stews or frying them, you can create your own fresh paprika powder, which puts anything you can buy in a can or bottle, Hungarian or otherwise, to shame. You are assured, too, that it is made with a true Hungarian pepper with all its complex flavors. The paprika powder produced commercially in the United States is actually made with chili peppers of the New Mexico pod type—good peppers, but as Peter Kopcinski says, they "lack the flavor, balance, and bouquet" you get with true Hungarian paprika peppers.

Varieties

'Boldog': 55 days green, 80 days crimson red, sweet Hungarian spice pepper with a slight bite, early short-season pepper that keeps on producing. Peter Kopcinski says, "So good fresh—like an explosion of flavor in your mouth."

'Giant Szegedi' ('Sunshine,' 'Szegedi'): 70 days, 6-by-3-inch pods ripen from pale yellow to deep orange, classic Hungarian stuffing pepper, sweet, thick flesh, verticillium wilt tolerant

'Kalocsa': 72 days, green to red, Hungarian spice paprika, slender 5-by-1-inch pods, plants 2 feet tall, prime home garden variety in Hungary, mild, delicious paprika powder

Paprika (sweet paprika, Hungarian spice pepper): 100 days, red, 5-by-1-inch flattened fruits, mildly pungent, ideal for drying and grinding into a powder

How to prepare: The meaty "vegetable" paprikas are often fried with onions and spices and served as a side dish, added to soups and stews, or filled with rice or meat stuffings. In a Greek restaurant, I was served a dip with feta cheese, roasted fresh paprika peppers, and olive oil with warm pita bread, and it was to die for.

Spice paprika pods are usually dried and ground into powder that is used in classic Hungarian dishes like tomato soup with sour cream; paprika gravy for dumplings and overstuffed cabbage

(Top): 'Giant Szedgi,' *(middle)*: 'Figaro,' *(bottom)*: 'Tequila Sunrise'

or roast pork; goulash; and chicken or veal paprikash. For information on drying and grinding paprika peppers, see page 73.

Try your fresh paprika over creamed onions or scalloped potatoes, season your paella and humus with it, combine it with other spices to create a dry-rub for ribs, or add it to a garden chili to add dimension to the pepper flavors.

Pimiento

Both *pimento* and *pimiento* (from the Spanish pimienta) are commonly used names for this pepper. It would be a crime to limit pimientos to their traditional use, as a stuffing in olives, as these are especially tasty, sweet, meaty peppers. The pods have a thick flesh and are often, but not always, heart-shaped. Some varieties are fluted, flattened cheese-type peppers. Pimientos range from 2 to 3 inches wide and 2 to 4 $\frac{1}{2}$ inches long. Pod color ranges from dark green to bright red when mature.

Varieties

'Chevena Chujski': 85 days; from green to red; pointed, 3 to 6 inches long, some heart-shaped; sweet, rather thin flesh; compact plants, excellent for containers (see "Winter Care of Peppers in Containers," page 38).

'Figaro': 68 days; green to red heirloom Italian pimiento; to 4 inch flattened, scalloped fruits with rich flavor; very thick flesh; strong, vigorous plants

Pimento (pimiento): 65 days, 3-inch heart-shaped red fruits

'Pimento Elite': 85 days to red, hybrid, oval fruit to 3 inches, prolific, resistant to TMV

'Red Hungarian Pimento': 70 days, green to red, hybrid, large cheese-type pepper to 3 $\frac{1}{2}$ inches, thick walled, sweet, juicy, usually eaten fresh in Hungarian condiments

'Yellow Hungarian Pimento': similar to the one above except yellow, Renee's Garden offers a sampler package with both.

How to prepare: You can use pimientos in any recipe that calls for bell peppers either raw or cooked. I find they have more flavor than most bells, and the smooth skin is among the easiest to roast and peel. I enjoy them raw, cut up in a pasta or green salad, minced in corn bread and corn chowder, and they can be stuffed with a cold salad or hollowed out and used to hold a dip. Try them pickled as well. Roasted, peeled, and cut into strips, they have a great sweet flavor to add to a crunchy baguette sandwich filled with tomatoes, basil, anchovies, and I especially love to serve them in a roasted red pepper soup, for which you will find a recipe on page 83.

OTHER, SWEET

In this category I have included a variety of types, including the sweet banana and cherry peppers. Banana and cherry peppers include both sweet and hot varieties, and both are great for pickling. For information on the hot varieties, see the following listings.

As their name implies, cherry peppers are small, round, and look like cherries. The pods can reach 2 inches across. They are green when immature and turn red when mature. The pods are held erect on the plants.

Varieties

'Antohi Romanian': 53 days pale yellow, 78 days red, 4-by-2-inch tapered fruit, brought from Romania in 1991, delicious cooked, available from Johnny's Selected Seeds

'Red Cherry': 80 days, green maturing to red, small, round, 1 to 1 $\frac{1}{2}$ inches, perfect for pickling, compact plants

'Shishito' (Japanese sweet, 'Shishitou'): green to red, 2 $\frac{1}{2}$ inches long, nonpungent, available from Evergreen Y. H. Enterprises

'Golden Arrow': 58 days; early, very large, 8-inch-long golden sweet banana pepper; large shoulders; thick, crispy flesh; productive. Pepper breeder Peter Kopcinski says this is "an absolutely beautiful pepper baked or stuffed."

'Sweet Banana': 72 days, yellow to red, thick walled, conical, 2 to 8 inches long, waxy pods, sweet and mild, compact, prolific plants, susceptible to southern blight disease in warm, humid regions

'Tequila Sunrise': 77 days, green to orange, sweet fruits 5 inches long and 1 inch wide, borne upright on this productive plant, carried by Southern Exposure Seed Exchange

How to prepare: All of the banana-type peppers can be used in the yellow stage for pickles. They are tasty in salads, omelets, and sauces. The larger sweet banana peppers are good stuffed, fried, or baked. Cherry peppers are perfect for pickling, as described on page 70, and can be used raw in salads. In Italy, cherry peppers both hot and sweet are stuffed with cheese and prosciutto, marinated and served as antipasti. A recipe is on page 78. 'Shishito' (Japanese sweet) peppers are used in Japan raw in salads and tempura, cooked in a beef stir-fry, or pickled.

HOT

Though thought of as hot peppers, many of the chilies, such as the ancho peppers, are really quite mild. Some, on the other hand, like habaneros and Scotch bonnets, can be so hot folks wear gloves when harvesting them.

Ancho
(also called poblano, pasilla, and mulato)

There is much confusion about the category of chili peppers known as anchos. Ancho peppers are among the many covered by the name poblano when they are green. In Mexico, this same pepper, when dried, is referred to as an ancho, though most American growers and seed suppliers use the term ancho for the fresh green pods as well as the dried ones. These generally wedge-shaped peppers are 3 to 5 inches long and 2 to 4 inches wide at the shoulders, though there is variability in size and shape. When immature the fruits are dark green, almost black, but with maturity they turn red.

Varieties

Ancho/poblano: 80 days, dark green pear-shaped fruits, rich, meaty, essence-of-pepper flavor, use stuffed or roasted

'Ancho 101': 68 days green, 88 days red, medium hot thin-fleshed fruits 3 to 4 inches long; tall, rangy plants, best adapted to hot climates

'Ancho Mulatto' ('Mulato'): very dark brown when ripe, large, to 5 inches long and 3 inches across, fairly spicy, great flavor, used for stuffing

'Ancho Ranchero': 70 days, ripens to

Ancho

red, hybrid, very large fruits, large size makes easier to roast and peel

How to prepare: I've had my ancho pepper harvest vary from mildly hot to blazo, sometimes even in the same season. The spiciness seems to be influenced by the seed source, climate, and how much water they received.

In my own experience, and in talking to other chili mavens, ancho peppers are among the most choice and flavorful of the chilies. They have been a favorite in Mexico and the Southwest for centuries.

Anchos are not generally used raw and are most commonly harvested and cooked in their green stage. Their fairly tough skin is routinely roasted and peeled before using. Once peeled, the milder versions can be stuffed with cheese or meat for rellenos, and both the mild and hot ones can be cut up and used in vegetable dishes, casseroles, sauces, or chili. Strips of roasted ancho peppers (called *rajas*) are

stewed in sour cream to make *Rajas* (see page 69), wrapped with cheese in a warm tortilla for a heavenly snack, or added to burritos, tamales, and tacos. In Mexico, they are added to *arroz verde* (green rice), where they are combined with chicken broth and cilantro; stewed along with *nopalitos* (cactus pads) and pork; and often used in a traditional mole. Mole is a traditional dusky, complex sauce made with spices, vegetables, peppers, and usually chocolate. All sorts of variations are possible, including ones with ground pumpkin seeds. Moles traditionally accompany chicken, turkey, or meat.

Roasted fresh anchos are pureed for sauces and can be swirled into a cream of pepper soup, as described in the recipe on page 83, or poured to make a pool topped with stuffed squash blossoms, as described on page 80. Most good Mexican cookbooks have numerous recipes for anchos. They can also be frozen as you would the New Mexico type peppers and used interchangeably in most of their recipes. Be aware, though, that while the anchos give a deeper, more complex flavor, they also definitely give more kick.

In their dried form, anchos are reconstituted in boiling water and ground to a paste for the basis of numerous traditional Mexican salsas and stews, including chicken or turkey moles.

Banana/Wax

Banana peppers originated in Hungary, beginning with the Hungarian hot wax banana pepper, which was favored for many years because, among other reasons, it was the earliest and it could be enjoyed until the later ripening varieties came along. In the 1920s, sweet banana peppers were developed in Hungary, and the breeders created new varieties. Today, banana pepper pods, which are conical, range from 2 to 8 inches long and come in various shades of pale yellow when immature to red when ripe. Plants tend to be compact.

As with many types of peppers, which banana pepper is "best"—and the stage at which it is best to pick them—depends on cultural preferences. Hungarians, as a rule, tend to prefer short stuffing banana peppers that are sweet or semihot and picked at the immature yellow stage. Peter Kopcinski, on the other hand, likes them best when they are "just breaking with a bit of blush." Banana peppers are usually not eaten in the red stage.

Varieties

'Bulgarian Carrot' ('Shipkas'): 68 days, green to bright orange, quite hot; 3

Hungarian hot wax

$^1/_2$ inches long, intense fruity flavor, productive 18-inch plants, seed came from Bulgaria before the fall of the Iron Curtain, very susceptible to bacterial spot so not for hot, humid areas

Hungarian hot wax banana (Hungarian yellow wax hot, Hungarian wax, and several other variations on the name): 65 days, light green to yellow, mildly hot, to 8 inches long, banana-shaped fruits, strong plants to 2 feet, one of the best hot peppers for cooler climates

How to prepare: While generally eaten in their yellow stage, most banana peppers turn red when fully ripe. The 'Bulgarian Carrot' is harvested and eaten fresh in its orange stage. Both types have fairly thick walls, dry poorly, but are great for pickles, cut up and sprinkled over salads, or stuffed. They are also used in chutneys, marinades, and salsas. The Totally Tomatoes catalog states that 'Bulgarian

'Fajita' bell

Carrot' adds a delicious tint to jellies and its fruity flavors blend well in mango and pineapple salsas served with grilled fish or poultry.

Bell, spicy

The spicy bells are similar to sweet bell peppers except that they have been bred to be mildly pungent.

'Fajita': 68 days green, 80 days red, hybrid, 4-by-3 $^1/_2$-inch fruit, mildly pungent taste good for fajitas, compact plants

'Mexibell': 70 days, green to chocolate brown to red, All-American in 1988, a mildly pungent bell (500 Scoville units or less), good at any stage, TMV tolerant, available from Totally Tomatoes. 'Mexibell Improved,' which is hotter, is available from Tomato Growers Supply Company.

How to prepare: Use these peppers anywhere you would use a bell pepper if you want a little added heat.

Cayenne

This category of peppers is the primary one used in Creole and Cajun cooking and is also familiar to us when we buy it in powdered form as cayenne or hot pepper. In this category I am also including the Asian hot peppers because evidence suggests that many evolved from similar types, they often look quite similar, and they have the same flavor and heat.

The cayenne-types are among the hottest peppers commonly grown in the home garden, measuring between 30,000 and 50,000 Scoville units. The plants are up to 3 feet tall, multi-stemmed, and prolific. The fruits are most often narrow and wrinkled and range from 4 to 10 inches long, depending on the variety. Immature peppers are medium green and can be used fresh at this stage in spicy salsas. They are usually used in the ripe red stage dried for powder or flakes. The red mature fruits are often strung together and hung in kitchens for use and decoration.

Clockwise from above left: Cayenne, 'Thick Red Cayenne' 'Golden Cayenne' and 'Thai Dragon'

Varieties

Cayenne: 75 days, dark green to red, very hot, 6-inch pendant variable fruits depending on the seed company

'Golden Cayenne' ('Yellow Cajun Cayenne'): 65 days, dark green to golden yellow fruits, productive, stays yellow when dried

'Large Red Thick Cayenne' ('Large Thick Cayenne'): 76 days, wrinkled, 6-by-1 ¼-inch pendant fruits, very pungent; great for blazo sauce or for drying if split open

'Purple Cajun Cayenne': green ripening to purple, darkens when dried, carried by Renee's Garden as part of her Cajun Hot Cayennes mix

'Thai Dragon': 70 days, similar to 'Thai Hot' but larger hybrid, fruit 3 ½ inches long, tall plant, easily dried

'Thai Hot': 80 days, green to red, both colors on plant at same time, from Thailand, small, thin pods 1 to 1 ½ inches long, extremely hot, grows well in warmer regions

How to prepare: Cayenne types are used to provide a clear, intense hotness without complex pepper-flavor overtones. Don't look for fruity and musky flavors here—it's heat we're talking about. While not traditional, I use the classic cayennes and the Asian hot peppers interchangeably in recipes. Seedswoman Renee Shepherd combines the dried purple, red, and yellow cayennes as a hot confetti for salsas and to sprinkle over pizza. I find that this category of peppers works well in many Turkish, Greek, Middle Eastern, and African dishes. One dish in particular features peppers of this ilk: *harissa,* a traditional North African condiment or basting sauce, combines olive oil with ground cumin, cinnamon, coriander, caraway, and hot peppers, and it's served with couscous.

These peppers are primarily used in their red-ripe state, either fresh or dried. Cayennes are traditionally used to give gumbos, jambalaya, and Creole dishes their special spiciness and are a favorite for vinegars and oils. Cayennes are dried and chopped to produce spicy flakes that are added to Italian sausages and minestrone soups. In Italy, spicy peppers such as the cayennes are used to add a kick to soups, pasta dishes, seafood, and stews, especially in the south. In Asia, cayenne-type peppers are used in satay sauces, curries, and in a yogurt marinade for tandoori chicken.

Throughout much of southern China, Korea, India, and most of Southeast Asia, hot peppers yield the spiciness characteristic of many dishes such as stir-fries, curries, kim chee, marinades for seafood and poultry, and hot and spicy soups. Hot oils made by simmering peanut oil with cayenne or similar pepper flakes are used to flavor

stir-fries, as are pastes made by reconstituting similar peppers.

In much of Southeast Asia, long, thin red chili peppers are slivered lengthwise from below the stem to the end and then placed in ice water for a half hour until they open up and the slices form the petals of a flower.

Jalapeños

(called chile gordo *in Mexico)*
Jalapeños are medium-hot to hot peppers originating in Mexico and still widely used there today. They can be sold under the generic name jalapeño, though there are cultivated varieties such as 'Jalapeño Frienza,' which bears earlier, and a much milder form, 'Jalapeño TAM.'

Jalapeños as a group are quite similar in shape and size, all being fairly thick walled and ranging from 1 1/2 to 3 inches long and about 1 inch across. The immature pods are pendant on the plant, about 3 inches long and 1 inch wide, dark green ripening to red, and often have thin, netted markings

on the surface of the pods. Jalapeños can be hot, measuring between 2,500 and 10,000 Scoville units. They are most often harvested when they are dark green, but occasionally some are allowed to ripen for special uses. In this category I have also included two other thick-walled peppers, 'Fresno' and 'Santa Fe Grande,' as they are served in a similar way to jalapeños.

Varieties

'Fresno': 75 days, green to red, medium hot, upright fruits 2 to 3 inches long, spicy

Jalapeño: 75 days, best when green, will ripen to red, small, hot, thick-walled fruits of variable flavor depending on the seed company

'Jalapeño Frienza': 67 days, dark green to bright red, hybrid, early, large, to 3 1/2 inches long, medium hot, high yields, 2 feet tall, fruits all season

'Jalapeño TAM': 70 days, one-third as hot as the standard jalapeño, good for nachos

'Paul's Piñata' *(left)*,
'Jalapeño Frienza' *(right)*

'Santa Fe Grande'

'Jaloro': 75 days, bright yellow fruits turn red when ripe, great hot taste

'Paul's Piñata' ('NuMex Piñata'): a colorful jalapeño that goes from lime green to yellow to orange to red. Renee Shepherd of Renee's Garden named this pepper in honor of Dr. Paul Bosland, who likes to use all its colors in a festive jalapeño corn bread.

'Pizza Pepper': 80 days, thick-walled, flavorful, very mild fruits, early, prolific, developed for the Northwest

'Santa Fe Grande' ('Caribe'): 100 days, yellow to orange to red, from mildly hot to very hot, 3 1/2 inches long, narrow, one of the best for pickling

'Senorita Hybrid': 60 days, dark green to red, larger, thick-fleshed, mild version of jalapeño, TMV resistant

How to prepare: Jalapeño-type peppers are popular pickled in sandwiches, salsas, and seafood dishes such as pickled jalapeños with crab and avocado. Fresh, they are great stuffed with cheese and grilled for an appetizer or sliced and sprinkled over nachos, in salads, or on pizzas. Try them chopped in quesadillas, burritos, tacos, or dips. East Indian cooks grate jalapeños to use in samosas (spicy turnovers), curries, and in stewed vegetable dishes. Jalapeño jelly has a following and is often served with soft cheeses and crackers.

Because the fruits are fleshy, they don't dry well unless they are smoked. Smoked jalapeños are called *chipotles*. When preserved in a tomato sauce, they are called *chipotles en adobo*. Both are sometimes available in Mexican markets. Chipotles are made from both green and red jalapeños. To make your own chipotles, follow the recipe on page 71. You'll find a recipe for chipotle mashed potatoes on page 85. Ground chipotle peppers add a smoky rich flavor as well as heat to roast meat, marinades, sauces, and condiments. Once you have chipotles on hand, you can't cook without them.

New Mexico/'Anaheims'

Because of their pod type, the New Mexico peppers are sometimes referred to as long green or long red chilies. Varieties include several developed at New Mexico State University and the 'Anaheim.' This category of peppers is the backbone of the American chili-pepper industry.

Enjoyed in northern Mexico and known there as *chile verde*, these long green chili peppers have been cultivated in New Mexico for 300 years. Professor Fabian Garcia, a horticulturist at what is now New Mexico State University, developed the New Mexico

'Anaheim'

pod type from these peppers. Reportedly, he was on a quest for a mild chili pepper that would appeal to non-Hispanics. After years of breeding, the first one to be offered to the public was 'New Mexico #9' in 1917. New Mexico State University has been active in pepper research ever since. The older cultivars of long green chilis are called New Mexico; newer ones, NuMex. In 1896, Emilio Ortega took pepper seeds from New Mexico to his farm near Anaheim, California, eventually resulting in the 'Anaheim' variety, as well as the Ortega company, well known for their canned peppers.

Today, thousands of tons of the New Mexico peppers are grown in Hatch, New Mexico, and are sometimes referred to as Hatch peppers. The 'Anaheim' and New Mexico fruits are long and narrow, generally reaching 7 inches in length and 1 to 1 1/2 inches in width. One variety, 'NuMex Big Jim,' is especially long. 'Anaheim' and all of the New Mexico varieties are open pollinated. When immature,

'Big Chile'

'Sugarchile'

'Big Chile': 60 days green, 80 days red, hybrid, large, long fruits, early, widely adapted, good for cool-summer areas

'Espanola Improved': 70 days green, soon ripens to red, medium hot, to 5 inches long, New Mexico type, thin walled, good fresh or dried, prolific, recommended for Northeast gardens

'Magic Red': 60 days green, 85 red, hybrid, fruits 5 by $3/4$ inches, tapered, medium hot, great for drying, tall plants, widely adapted

'NuMex Big Jim' ('New Mex Big Jim'): 80 days, green to red, tapered, 6 to 13 inches long, medium hot, best in Southwest

'NuMex Joe E. Parker': 65 days, green to red, used in both stages, to 7-inch pods, mild, 2 $1/2$-foot plants, early, productive, Paul Bosland's favorite for rellenos, good reviews from New Mexico chefs and growers as well

'NuMex Mirasol': 100 days, green to red, medium-hot, 4-inch pods held erect, unique fruity flavor, prolific. Paul Bosland likes this for chili powder.

'Sugarchile': 60 days, green to red, hybrid, thick, sweet flesh with hot interior ribs, medium-long fruit, medium-size plant with heavy yield, widely adapted

How to prepare: Often roasted and peeled when green, or dried when red-ripe, the long green/red chilies are characteristic of southwestern-style foods. The peeled strips are added to casseroles, soups, and stewed beans; used in quesadillas, enchiladas, chilies, and chicken and bean burritos; stewed

most of these peppers are light green ripening to crimson; a few ripen to yellow, orange, or chocolate brown. Their pungency varies from mild to hot, depending on the cultivar and growing conditions. In their ripe state, they are often strung and dried to make what is called a *ristra*. In the United States, most commercial paprika powder is actually made from peppers of the New Mexico type.

Some resources say that 'Anaheim' and the New Mexico peppers do not do well in the Northeast. Dr. Paul Bosland, professor at New Mexico State University, says that they will produce green peppers, but most won't have time to ripen. Exceptions are 'Espanola Improved' and 'Big Chili,' noted below. A seed company in New Mexico, Enchanted Seeds, carries many NuMex varieties.

Varieties

'Anaheim': 75 days, green to red, 7 inches long, mildly pungent, used fresh or dried

in sour cream for tacos, braised with pork, used in corn and squash tamales, scrambled eggs, and corn bread.

Roasted and peeled strips and whole peppers freeze well in plastic freezer bags. I thaw the pepper strips all winter to use in veggieburgers, salsas, burritos, scrambled eggs, and over nachos.

Ripe New Mexico peppers have thin skins and can be dried on ristras or in a dehydrator. The dried peppers can be reconstituted with boiling water and ground with a mortar and pestle to make a paste to add to sauces. In addition, they can be ground in a spice grinder to make a mild red chili powder used to season cooked sauces for numerous meat dishes. When used in chili con carne or other stews and sauces, it is usually combined with other varieties of ground chili powders and spices because New Mexico–style peppers are rather one-dimensional in flavor and have little heat.

'Aurora'

'Fiesta'

'Super Chili'

Ornamental Peppers

Ornamental peppers are particularly striking or colorful, usually quite small-podded pepper plants. Ornamental peppers can be used for culinary purposes, though they often have the heat but not the distinctive flavor that other peppers do. Of course, many of the hot or sweet peppers grown for culinary use are also quite ornamental. As a rule, these plants are smaller than most of the bells and hot peppers.

Varieties

'Aurora': 75 days, small green to lavender to orange to red pods, hot, compact plant, use for borders, available from Southern Exposure Seed Exchange

'Fiesta' ('Christmas'): 90 days, hot, slim, 2-by-1/4-inch white to bright red fruit cluster above the foliage of small, compact plant

'Poinsettia': 65–90 days, green to purple to red, plants 1 1/2 to 2 feet tall bear pointed fruits 2 to 3 inches long by about 1/4 inch wide, growing upright in clusters. There is confusion about this pepper as Burpee sells one and pods are rounded.

'Super Chili': 75 days, green to orange to red, hybrid, 2 1/2-inch cone-shaped fruits with thin hot flesh, semicompact plants that are showy, great in containers, prolific

'Variegata' ('Varingata,' 'Tri-Color Variegata,' purple variegated): 90 days, green and purple, maturing to red, hot; about 1-inch-long oval fruits, beautiful plant with variegated green, white, and purple leaves and purple and white blossoms

'Yellow Ornamental': bright yellow, spicy, hot fruits to 1 1/2 inches long, upright. Keep your eye out for this pepper, it's gorgeous. I've only seen it sold in florist shops.

How to prepare: Use these peppers where you would use a cayenne, but taste them first as some ornamental peppers can be very hot, others slightly bitter.

Paprika, hot

Paprikas are often considered sweet, even though they may have a bit of pungency. Others have enough heat to land them in the definitely hot category.

Varieties

'Almapaprika': 65 days, white to red, Hungarian vegetable paprika, 1 1/2-by-2-inch fruits, thick, crunchy, medium-hot flesh

'Paprika Supreme': 70 days green, 80 days red ripe, hybrid, sweet and slightly spicy, good fresh or dried for paprika powder, 6 to 8 inches long, 1 1/2-inch-wide tapered fruits, widely adapted

'Almapaprika' *(above)*, 'Paprika Supreme'
(below)

How to prepare: Use these peppers
the same way you would the sweet
paprikas when you want a little heat.

Pasilla

While there is a pasilla pepper type,
the word *pasilla* is also sometimes used
in reference to ancho peppers. *Pasilla*
means "little raisin" in Spanish. These
peppers, however, are not small and
round but long, from about 3 to 12
inches, and slender, about 1 inch wide.
The name is due to the wrinkled, dark
brown appearance of the skin when
they are ripe and to their raisinlike
aroma. (Pasilla peppers are also called
chilaca when green.) Pasilla peppers
are mildly pungent, about 1,000 or
more Scoville units. The plants have an
upright growth habit, to about 3 feet.
Flowers are white.

Varieties

'Pasilla Bajillo' (chilaca, chile negro):
80 days, dark green maturing to
dark brown, to 10 inches long,
cylindrical pods, fruity flavor and
almost no heat, strong upright
plants, heavy yields, TMV resistant

'Pasilla de Oaxaca': brown when ripe,
medium-size pods, mild, available
from Enchanted Seeds

How to prepare: Pasillas are primarily used dried and ground for
their rich smoky, fruity flavors. Use
these peppers where you need a flavorful dried pepper for added dimension. Chef Mark Miller describes them
as one of the "holy trinity" of chilies
used in a traditional Mexican mole
along with anchos and mulatos.
Pasillas are also used in other sauces,
with seafood, and in dishes such as
soups and stews. Try ground pasilla
peppers mixed with salt to make a dip
for slices of jicama. Sometimes,
ground pasilla peppers are combined
with much hotter dried peppers.

Round, hot

There are various small, hot cherrylike
peppers. Pods are from 1 to 2 inches
across, green when immature, and
from orange to red when mature. The
pods are held erect on the plants,
which grow up to 2 feet tall. The fruits
range from very mild to about 3,500
Scoville units.

Varieties

'Ammazzo' ('Joe's Round'): 65 days
green, 90 days red, small Italian hot
pepper borne in clusters, tall ornamental plant, carried by Southern
Exposure Seed Exchange

'Cascabel': 90 days, dark green to red-
dish-brown, Mexican, very pungent,
round 1-inch pods, usually used
dried

'Large Red Cherry Hot': 78 days, red
cherry-sized peppers, perfect for
pickling, mild to medium hot

How to prepare: Most cherry peppers are great for pickling. If you want
especially spicy pickles, combine them

'Pasilla Bajillo,' *(left)*; 'Ammazzo' *(right)*

57

with jalapeños or serranos. Try them Italian style stuffed with cheese and prosciutto and marinated, as in the recipe on page 78. 'Cascabel' is occasionally enjoyed fresh, but it is more often dried and used in Mexican sauces, stews, and salsas.

Serranos

Serrano peppers are among the most popular of the fresh chili peppers used in Mexico and the American Southwest. The fruits are an inch or so long and a little more than $1/2$ wide. They are green when immature, ripen to red, and are used in both stages. I prefer to let them ripen, which brings out their distinctive rich, almost sweet flavor. Serranos are quite hot, measuring from 7,000 to 25,000 Scoville units. The name *serrano* means "from the highlands." I've had success bringing them through the winter if we only have light frosts and cover the plants with floating row

covers midwinter. The plants have gray-green leaves and are striking when covered with ripe fruit.

Varieties

Serrano: 80 days, green to red, 2 inches long, rich, hot flavor, 3-foot-tall, upright plants

'Purple Serrano': 85 days, fruits ripen to a beautiful deep purple, otherwise very similar to the red serrano

'Super Serrano': 60 days green, 80 days red, very hot, productive in Northeast gardens

How to prepare: Serrano peppers are quite hot and wonderful used fresh in really spicy salsas, guacamole, and in cooked dishes such as chili, eggs, beans, and other vegetable dishes. They can also be pickled or dried as they are fairly thin walled. Dried serranos may be ground up for use in chili powder. In Mexico, I've had serranos served to me on a little

plate to accompany a taco or burrito. They have been quickly fried in a little oil and have lots of flavor. In Mexico, pickled serranos are sometimes served with pickled onions and carrots, to accompany beer. In Texas, cooks using fresh peppers choose serranos when they want a dish to be quite hot; for a milder dish—perhaps to serve a visitor to Texas—they generally choose the jalapeño.

Tree Peppers

Mexican people consider the chili de árbol one of the best of the very hot peppers. Similar to cayennes, the fruits are about 2 $1/2$ inches long and $1/2$ inch wide. They are light green when immature and red when ripe. These peppers can also be grown as house-plants.

Varieties

Chili de árbol (chili de arbol, 'Chili D'Arbol,' tree chili): green to red, pods 1 to 2 $1/2$ inches long by $1/2$ inch across, very hot, plants upright to 6 feet

How to prepare: Chili de árbol can be substituted when you want the hotness of a cayenne but would enjoy some subtle chili overtones. It's analogous to using brandy instead of distilled alcohol. Chili de árbol is used with meats, in chili, in salsas—whenever you need a very hot pepper.

Ripe Serranos

CAPSICUM ANNUUM VAR. AVICULARE

Bird Peppers

THE TERM *BIRD PEPPERS* IS A common name often used when referring to various wild species of peppers or to their pods, including those of the species *Capsicum annuum* var. *aviculare*. Certain small-podded domesticated versions of wild peppers are also sometimes referred to as bird peppers. In addition, some peppers with very small pods have bird pepper as part of their names, such as the Trinidad bird pepper. Bird peppers are tiny, often about the size of a pea, and fiery hot. The name comes from the fact that the fruits are a favorite of certain species of birds, which are the main propagators of the seed. Seeds tend to be slow to germinate (can take from 3 to 12 weeks). These peppers need a long hot growing season. Plants take from 90 to 200 days to mature, but the good news is that they may be grown in containers and brought inside in winter or grown in greenhouses.

The most well-known of the wild peppers are called chiltepíns. They grow as a wild shrub in Mexico and parts of southern Arizona and Texas. In the wild, chiltepíns grow in transition zones between mountains and deserts, underneath "nurse" trees such as the mesquite, which protect them from the harsh sunlight. Chiltepíns are some of the hottest peppers, measuring

'Chiltepíns'

from 50,000 to 100,000 Scoville units, though there are some who claim the heat is fleeting, and it is the chiltepíns' special flavor for which they are prized. Chiltepíns are attractive plants and can be grown as perennials in areas of the low desert with shade or filtered light. They also do well in containers. Mature pods should be protected from birds, especially mockingbirds.

Luckily for birds, the ripe fruits of wild peppers separate easily from the plant. According to Dr. Bosland, when the Native Americans, and later breeders, began developing peppers, they bred for fruit that would not fall off easily. These are referred to as domesticated peppers. Some domesticated peppers have then naturalized and so are again picked as "wild" peppers.

Today, says Dr. Bosland, the term *chiltepíns* usually refers to the small round-podded peppers, and the term *chilipiquíns* is commonly used to refer to the "bullet-shaped, pointed" peppers. Both can be found in wild and domesticated forms.

Varieties

Different varieties of chiltepíns are named for the region where the seed was collected. Native Seeds/SEARCH has the most extensive selection of chiltepíns available.

Chiltepín (tepin, chiltecpin): green to red, hot, very tiny, usually round pods, though some offerings may be the elongated pods; plants average 4 feet; available from Redwood City Seed Company, Tomato Growers

Supply Company, and Native Seeds/SEARCH

'Chiltepín Tarahumara': high-yielding, produces lots of tiny round red peppers, dependable, available from Native Seeds/SEARCH

Chilipiquín (piquín, pequín): green to red, quite hot, elongated ¹/₂-inch pods (up to 3 inches on plants in home gardens), pods may be erect above the plant or pendant, available from Redwood City Seed Company, J. L. Hudson, and The Pepper Gal

'NuMex Bailey Piquin Chile': 120 days, from New Mexico State University Chile Pepper Breeding Program, tall, columnar plants bearing small, oblong fruit, fruits fall off at maturity, extremely hot, available from Tomato Growers Supply Company

How to prepare: Despite their size, bird peppers pack a real wallop and should only be used when a very hot pepper is desired. The pods are usually dried, then ground; use a mask and grind them outside or they will seriously affect your eyes and breathing. They can also be used in hot sauces or crushed with beans in soups and stews.

Sometimes bird peppers are combined with a milder but very flavorful chili pepper such as an ancho. In Africa, bird peppers are used to make a paste, then added to lamb stew, sauces, and peanut soup; or to make jerky.

CAPSICUM BACCATUM

THE PEPPERS OF *CAPSICUM baccatum* are commonly called *aji* in South America, and most cultivated peppers with aji in their name are *C. baccatum,* though not all of them. *C. baccatum* probably originated in Bolivia or Peru. It was domesticated and developed by the pre-Incan peoples and today is still very popular in Peru as well as other parts of South America. The plants tend to be tall, up to 5 feet, have large green leaves, and can be very prolific. The pods are usually long and narrow, ranging from 3 to 6 inches long and about 1 to 1 ¹/2 inches wide, though they can be round and even habanero-shaped. They are usually very hot, ranging from 30,000 to 50,000 Scoville units. The pods are usually green when they are immature, ripening to orange-red. However, they can ripen to yellow or brown. They can take up to 120 days to ripen. Flowers have white petals with yellow, green, or brown spots and yellow anthers.

Varieties

'Aji Colorado' ('Aji Red'): 90 days, orange-red when ripe, to 5 inches long, very hot

'Aji Cristal': 90 days, pale yellow 4-inch fruits mature to red, medium hot

'Peri-Peri': 100 days, green to orange or red, 2 inches long by 2 ¹/2 inches wide, mild pungency, flavorful, taken from South America to Portugal, unusual shape similar to habañero, vinelike plant

How to prepare: These peppers are usually quite hot, have a fruity flavor, and are good fresh in salsas, mixed with lime juice, and in ceviche (lime-marinated fish). Aji pods can be dried and crushed into a very spicy powder that's good with chicken. Be sure to use gloves and a mask when grinding them.

'Aji Cristal'

CAPSICUM CHINENSE

DESPITE ITS NAME, *CAPSICUM chinense* originated in the Amazon basin, not China. From there the species was taken to the Caribbean, where different land races of *C. chinense* were developed on various islands. These incredibly spicy peppers became important in the cuisine of the different islands and were given local names. Today, there is great variety within *C. chinense*, in both pod shape and levels, which range from 0 to 577,000 Scoville units. The plants are usually from 1 to 4 feet tall, though they can be taller. The pods range from tiny pea-size fruits to 5 inches long; some are quite wrinkled. They are green when immature and ripen to yellow, orange, red, brown, or even white. They are quite flavorful, with a distinctive fruity (some say smoky) taste and aroma. The flowers are white or green and have purple anthers. *C. chinense* is said to do best in areas of high humidity and warm nights. But I have had excellent results growing habañeros in my northern California garden despite our low nighttime summer temperatures (around 50°F).

Habañero means "from Havana," and the plant may have migrated from the Caribbean to Mexico at some time in its history. Most gardeners and cooks are familiar with the orange habanero from the Yucatán Peninsula, but there are habañeros of all colors. The pods are usually 1 1/2 to 2 1/2 inches long and 1 to 1 1/2 inches wide.

Reputedly, the hottest *C. chinense* is 'Red Savina,' which tips the scale at a scorching 577,000 Scoville units. Another familiar variety, the Scotch Bonnet, comes from Jamaica. Scotch Bonnet has pods that tend to be a bit smaller than the habañero and more wrinkled; they are green when immature, ripening to yellow or red.

'Caribbean Red Habañero,' *(above)*, 'Habañero' *(left)*

Varieties

'Aji Dulce': 110 days, green to orange-red to red, heirloom from Venezuela, flavor and aroma of habañero but only trace of heat, recommended for the South, needs long growing season, available from Southern Exposure Seed Exchange

'Caribbean Red Habañero': 75 days green, 100 days red, light green ripening to deep red, pods 1 ½ inches long, extremely hot

'Chocolate Habañero': 100 days, yellow-green to reddish brown to chocolate brown, heirloom, aromatic, fiery fruits, tall, spreading plants with good foliage cover, recommended for the South, needs long growing season, carried by Southern Exposure Seed Exchange

'Habañero': 85–100 days, green to true orange, 1 to 2 ½ inches long, 1 inch wide, extremely hot, use carefully, ornamental plant

How to prepare: Handle these peppers carefully. I find I must wear gloves to protect myself from burns. Use the minced raw peppers sparingly in tomato salsa cruda (fresh salsas) and fruit salsas. A small amount goes a long way in soups, Caribbean curries, marinades, vinegars, and jerk sauces. Sometimes habañeros are used with seafood and in ceviches. They can be dried for chili powder, but if you do, wear a protective mask when grinding the peppers.

CAPSICUM FRUTESCENS

THE MOST COMMONLY GROWN *Capsicum frutescens* is tabasco, the pepper used by the McIlhenny Company on Avery Island, Louisiana, for making their famous Tabasco sauce. *C. frutescens* needs very warm long summers to produce well. The plants are from 1 to 4 feet tall; the flowers are greenish white. The pods are about 1 ½ to 4 inches long by ½ inch wide. They are yellow, purple, or green, ripening to red, and can be numerous. The pods are held erect above the foliage, making for a very attractive plant. Fruits are rated between 55,000 and 80,000 Scoville units.

Varieties

'Bolivian Rainbow': 75 days, purple, yellow, and red fruits, very hot, beautiful tall plant with small purple leaves, early, very productive

'Greenleaf': 80 days, tabasco-type resistant to tobacco etch virus, best for the South and East

Tabasco: 80 days, light yellow-green to red, fiery hot, used to make Tabasco sauce, tall plants

'Yatsufusa' (chilies Japones or Japanese type): green to red, fruits 4 inches long, ¼ inch wide, borne on top in clusters of 6 or so peppers, hot and spicy, striking plant, popular in Asia and California, available from Redwood City Seed Company

'Bolivian Rainbow'

'Tobasco' *(above)*; 'Yatsufusa' *(below)*

CAPSICUM PUBESCENS

C. PUBESCENS HAS THE FEWEST cultivars of the domesticated pepper species. It is native to the Andes. The name comes from the pubescent (hairy) leaves. Unlike those of most peppers, the flowers are purple. The round pods are 3 inches long and 2 inches across. Coming from high mountain country, the plants require cooler weather than most peppers, though they won't survive hard freezes. They need bees and another plant of the same variety to be polli-nated and produce fruit, or they must be hand pollinated by the gardener. These hot peppers range from 30,000 to 50,000 Scoville units or higher.

How to prepare: These very spicy peppers are sometimes used fresh for salsas, curries, sauces, and in many dishes where cayennes are appropriate. Dried or made into a paste, they can be used to season stir-fries. Their most famous use is to flavor vinegar.

Varieties

'Rocoto' ('Manzano'): 90 to 180 days, in Mexico it's called *canario* when

'Canario' *(above)*;
'Mazano' blossom *(right)*

yellow; turns red when ripe, very hot, looks like a small apple, needs a long, moderate growing season such as in coastal U.S. areas

How to prepare: Use fresh in salsas or stuffed and baked. They have thick walls and do not dry well.

red hot harvest

In fall, most Americans think of apples, pumpkins, and brilliant foliage, but in New Mexico, the harvest celebration is spicy. With huge containers of chilies in the fields, ristras hanging everywhere to symbolize prosperity, even a Santa Fe Wine and Chile Fiesta, this state greets winter with a fiery in-your-face attitude.

From mid-September to mid-October, you can explore back roads from historic Mesilla in the south to Velarde in the north and join the harvest celebration. See chilies being harvested, visit farmers' markets to taste unusual chili varieties you can grow, and take home ristras of dried chilies, or roasted green ones to freeze. And of course, you will dine on chili dishes all along the way to get more recipe ideas. Take a walk on the wild side next fall and celebrate chilies in New Mexico.

Places to Visit

Hatch, New Mexico—Hatch, in the southern part of the state, is the center of chili growing in New Mexico. Acres of chili fields surround the town, and numerous stores sell chili-related gifts and foods as well as ristras of all types. The Hatch Chili Festival is held annually in September. Telephone the Hatch Chili Express at 505-267-3226 for more information. Old Highway 28 outside Hatch is scenic and takes you through chili country. Nearby Las Cruces holds a year-round farmers' market Wednesday and Saturday mornings in the downtown open-air mall, and numer-

ous stands offer chilies in many different forms.

Santa Fe, New Mexico—Santa Fe is situated in the mountains of north-

A fruit stand in northern New Mexico *(above and above center)* offers apples and chili ristras. Hatch, New Mexico *(below far right)* is the center of chili production for much of America. Chili ristras *(below center)* are hung from the rafters to signify prosperity.

with chilies, ristras, apples, and pumpkins. In Santa Fe, there is a great farmers' market on Saturday mornings. The Santa Fe Wine and Chili Fiesta is held annually in September. For more information on the farmer's market and fiesta, call the Santa Fe Visitor's Bureau at 800-777-2489.

ern New Mexico and is the jumping-off spot for more scenic harvest trips; namely, north to Taos, Chimayó, and Velarde. Farm stands abound, filled

cooking from the pepper garden

It's great to have a wealth of garden peppers. Pepper harvests start slowly in mid summer—usually beginning with a few early bells and jalapeños—but gather momentum until yields are finally slowed by cold weather. After you harvest your fresh peppers, store them in a paper bag in the refrigerator—they'll keep for up to two weeks.(If you store them in plastic bags they tend to rot.)

Sweet Peppers

To prepare bell peppers of all types, wash them and cut out the stem end. For stuffing them, cut a large whole in the top. For including them in salads or cooked dishes, slice the peppers in half and remove the seeds and

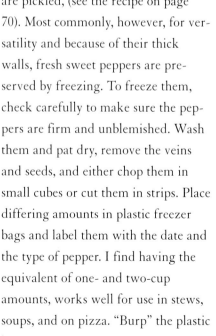

veins, then cut them in strips or chop them in the size needed for the recipe. (If the skins are tough, mince the peppers before using them or roast them and peel the skins off.) If you want to create rings, cut out the stem end, scoop out the seeds and veins and slice the pepper width-wise into appropriate size rings. Ripe peppers are the best for serving raw—unripe ones are best cooked.

There are a number or ways to preserve sweet peppers. Some sweet paprika varieties and a few of the thin-walled sweet peppers like 'Gypsy' can be cut in strips and dried in a

dehydrator. The paprika varieties are ground in a spice grinder, or in a coffee grinder used only for spices. The others are reconstituted with boiling water for ten minutes before being used in recipes calling for cooking peppers. Occasionally, sweet peppers are pickled, (see the recipe on page 70). Most commonly, however, for versatility and because of their thick walls, fresh sweet peppers are preserved by freezing. To freeze them, check carefully to make sure the peppers are firm and unblemished. Wash them and pat dry, remove the veins and seeds, and either chop them in small cubes or cut them in strips. Place differing amounts in plastic freezer bags and label them with the date and the type of pepper. I find having the equivalent of one- and two-cup amounts, works well for use in stews, soups, and on pizza. "Burp" the plastic bags to remove any extra air. My favorite frozen-pepper dishes use

Few garden treats so characterize the differences between store-bought and homegrown produce as fresh paprika *(opposite)*. 'Yankee Bell' peppers *(above)*.

roasted peppers that are peeled before freezing. I divide the roasted peppers in amounts suitable for say, a roasted-pepper soup, or a soubise sauce (see recipes on pages 83 and 84) and label them as such. I then have an "instant" soup or sauce ready all winter long. (See the following sections for information on roasting peppers.)

Hot Peppers

Preparing hot peppers calls for caution. To protect your hands from chemical burns use rubber gloves or purchase inexpensive, throw-away, latex gloves available from beauty or surgical-supply houses—they are less clumsy than rubber ones. And as always, make sure not to rub your eyes while working with spicy peppers. The heat in hot peppers is located in the placental tissue along the veins that support the seeds. If you want to lessen the hotness of peppers remove the veins and seeds.

Fresh, spicy peppers can be thinly sliced or minced and added raw to salsas, ceviche, and used in dressings or offered as a serve-yourself condiment. It is easier to evenly disperse the heat in a sauce or salsa if you mince peppers rather than cut them in large chunks. Besides being used raw, more commonly, hot peppers are sliced or diced and added to dishes that are to be cooked such as tamales, soups and sauces, or stuffed when whole and cooked in a batter.

Because the flesh of most hot peppers are thin, they are easily dried for winter use. Further, some of the hot varieties are arguably better tasting when dried. (See the interview with Doug Kaufmann on page 76 on the taste of dried peppers and for ways of reconstituting them for salsas.) Full-ripe peppers are the form most commonly dried, but green ones are also occasionally dried. If you live in an arid climate you can string and hang ripe, thin-walled hot peppers in a warm dry place. (For information, see page 27.) In humid or rainy climates, or if you are drying unripe hot peppers, they must be dried in either a dehydrator, in a gas oven using only the pilot light, or in an electric oven at 150°F for about 12 hours. In most cases it helps if you cut a slit in the side of the pepper, and if you rotate the peppers a number of times a day. (The tiny bird peppers however, are so easily dried they need only to be placed on a sunny windowsill for a few days.) Once your peppers are brittle-dry, to keep them dry and the insects under control, store them in a jar with a lid or in a sealable plastic bag. To reconstitute the dried peppers, wipe any dust off them, break them into a few pieces, and put them in a bowl and pour boiling water over them and let

them sit for about 20 minutes. They can then be ground into a paste and added to sauces or combined with garlic and other spices to create a mole or salsa. See the recipe for Salsa Cruda on page 75 for more information. All dried peppers can be ground as recommended for chili powder or paprika as described on page 73.

A great way to preserve the small hot peppers like the Thai and habañeros, is to pickle them. (see page 70.) The popular and thick-walled jalapeños can be preserved by blanching them in boiling water for two minutes, cooling them, and then freezing them in plastic freezer bags; or smoking and drying them, thus creating what are called chipotles. Directions for making chipotle are found on page 71. Other hot peppers, such as the 'Anaheims' and poblanos, can be roasted and peeled (see below) and frozen in freezer containers and are thus ready for rajas in seconds.

How to Roast Peppers

Char ripe peppers by holding them over a gas flame for a few minutes. Turn constantly till the skin blackens and blisters evenly. If you have an electric stove, put them under the broiler and char them the same way, or char them over a grill. Put charred peppers in a paper bag to steam for a few minutes. The point is to have the peppers roasted but still somewhat firm inside and to make the skins come off readily.

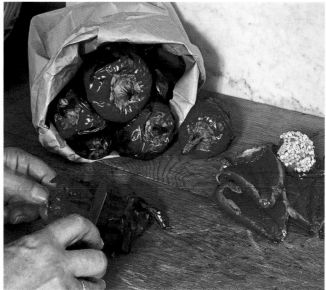

Then scrape or lightly rinse the skin off, remove the stem and seeds, and cut into strips. If your hands are sensitive, wear rubber gloves. To prevent burning your eyes, do not rub them while you work with chilies.

Marinated Roasted Pimientos

This recipe will become a part of your repertoire. There are so many ways to use these peppers to add zing to your sandwiches, soups, pasta dishes, and sauces that you'll find you can't cook without having them on hand. The roasted pepper strips will keep in the refrigerator for a week or so. The remaining olive oil can be added to marinades and dressings, but it must be kept refrigerated.

> About 12 large pimiento peppers
> 8 garlic cloves
> 3/4 to 1 cup extra virgin olive oil

Roast the peppers in the oven, under the broiler, or on the grill; then peel and remove the seeds and the stem end. Layer the peppers in a quart jar with a good seal.

Pour the oil in a sauté pan. Lightly crush the garlic cloves with the back of a chef's knife. Add the garlic cloves to the oil, and cook them slowly over low heat for about 5 minutes or until the garlic starts to turn golden. Drain the garlic from the oil, and slowly pour the oil over the peppers, occasionally running a rubber spatula carefully around the sides of the jar to allow the oil to fill all the air pockets, and then refrigerate.

A half hour before using your peppers, take out the quantity to be served and drain them. Let the peppers come to room temperature, and serve them as part of an antipasto or use in them in other recipes.

Makes 1 quart.

Rajas

Rajas, also called chili con crema, are a traditional Mexican way to serve roasted chili peppers, wonderful as a filling for an omelet or burritos. I was first introduced to this exquisite condi-ment by Craig Dremann of the Redwood City Seed Company.

> 12 green poblanos or ripe (red)
>   California or 'Anaheim' chilies
> 1 1/2 to 2 cups light sour cream
> 1/2 teaspoon minced fresh Mexican
>   or standard oregano

Roast the peppers according to the directions on page 68. Into the top half of a double boiler put the sour cream, roasted chili strips, and oregano, and stir to mix. Put the double boiler over simmering water and heat the mixture. Make sure not to let the water boil or the cream will curdle. The mixture is ready to serve when it is fairly warm but not simmering.

Serves 4.

How to Pickle Peppers

Pickle only fresh-picked unblemished peppers or you will have inferior pickles. To avoid cloudy pickle juice, don't use hard water. Note that iodized table salt may darken your pickles. Instead, use soft water and pickling salt or pure granulated salt. The proportions in the following recipes are high enough in acidity to be safe. Improperly prepared or processed pickles can be dangerous. If you are unfamiliar with the pickling or canning process, consult *The Joy of Cooking* or *The Complete Guide to Home Canning, Preserving, and Freezing* by the USDA for complete information.

To prepare your peppers, wash them well and drain. Use the directions in the following two recipes for the ingredient amounts. If you want to preserve your pickled peppers for more than a few weeks, you will need to can them using a special canning pot (a canner).

To can your pickled peppers, bring a large pot of water to the boil. Sterilize your canning jars by boiling them for 10 minutes. In a small saucepan, cover new canning lids with a few inches of water and bring the water to a boil. Keep both jars and lids at a simmer until you are ready to use them. While you are preparing the pickles, bring the canner to a boil with enough water in it to cover the jars by 1 inch.

Once you have filled your jars, wipe their tops with a clean damp towel to assure a tight seal. Put the lids on the jars, then screw on the canning rings, adjusting the rings so they are fairly tight. Process the pickled peppers in the canner, making sure the boiling water covers the jars by at least 1 inch. Follow the recommended processing time given in each recipe. Start to count the processing time from the time the hot jars are placed in the actively boiling water. If you are canning at more than 1,000 feet above sea level, consult the USDA tables for different canning times.

Remove the jars and set them upright, several inches apart, on a wire rack to cool. You will know that the jar is properly sealed when the lid makes a popping sound and if the lids are not easily removed. Any jars that have not sealed should be refrigerated and used within a month.

Pickled Cherry Peppers

Peppers are a perfect vegetable for pickling. Use these pickled peppers as a garnish for sandwiches and antipasto platters, or sprinkle them chopped over southwestern-style salads.

> About 1 pound red cherry peppers, hot or sweet
> 1 large green jalapeño pepper, sliced
> About 1 pint distilled white vinegar
> 1 teaspoon sea salt

Wash the peppers and trim the stems. Cut a slit in the side of each pepper to allow the liquid to enter. Pack the raw peppers in a sterilized 1-quart canning jar, distributing the jalapeño slices among the red cherry peppers. Bring the vinegar and salt to a boil in a small saucepan and pour it over the peppers.

You will need to displace all the air in the peppers with vinegar to allow the jar to be filled properly when processed. To release the air bubbles lodged between the peppers, use a chopstick or other long thin tool to gently nudge the peppers from side to side. In addition, use a spoon to press down gently on the peppers to release any air trapped inside.

Place the lid on the jar and refrigerate, using the peppers within one month. To preserve for a longer time, process them in a boiling water bath for 20 minutes, following the instructions with the canner.

Makes 1 quart.

Sweet Pickled Rainbow Bells

These pickles are great to serve with sandwiches, as a snack, or as part of an antipasto plate. They also make a welcome gift and are most decorative if the colorful pepper strips are arranged in a pleasing pattern in the canning jar. Spices such as cloves, cinnamon sticks, and star anise can be added to the jar to vary the recipe.

These peppers become soft and lose quality faster than many other types of pickles, so plan to use them within a

few months. When choosing your peppers, look for tall, brightly colored, firm peppers, each weighing about 6 ounces. (If you wish to preserve the peppers, follow the canning information given above and process them in pint jars for 10 minutes.)

1 large red bell pepper
1 large green bell pepper
1 large yellow bell pepper
1 large orange bell pepper
2 cups white wine vinegar
$1/4$ cup sugar
1 tablespoon salt

Remove the stems, veins, and seeds from the peppers, and slice them lengthwise into strips about 1 inch wide. Place the pepper strips in a large bowl, cover them with boiling water, and let stand for 5 minutes. Drain the peppers, and pack them standing up in two sterilized wide-mouth pint jars. Alternate the colors of the peppers around the outside of the jar to give a rainbow effect. The peppers for the middle of the jar can be arranged in a random manner.

In the meantime, pour the vinegar into a small saucepan and add the sugar and salt. Bring the mixture to a boil, stirring to dissolve the sugar. Pour the vinegar mixture over the peppers to within $1/2$ inch of the top. Carefully run a knife around the inside of the jar to release any air bubbles. Place the lid on the jar and refrigerate and use the peppers within one month.

Makes 2 pints.

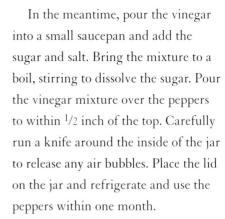

How to Make Chipotles

Chipotles are smoked red or green ripe jalapeño peppers. They look a bit like old wrinkled leather, but they are famous for their rich, smoky, complex flavors. Besides flavor, chipotles also pack some heat. A traditional way of preparing chipotles is to stew them in a mild red-chili sauce, which is called *adobo*. This flavorful mixture can be added to numerous Mexican dishes.

To use dried chipotles in a sauce or a cooked dish, first soften by pouring boiling water over them and let them soak for about 20 minutes. Then cut them up or purée them and add them to your recipe. You can also grind dried chipotles into a powder, which is a convenient way to add a smoky, hot dimension to a dish.

To smoke jalapeños you will need a smoker, or what is commonly called a Cajun cooker. A smoker is a metal box or cylinder with a charcoal pan at the bottom. Above the charcoal is a water pan, and above the water pan are

71

grilling racks for the peppers. Smokers are covered by a lid and usually come with a temperature gauge. Commercial smokers come with directions for basic smoking.

To make chipotles, half fill the pan in the bottom of the smoker with charcoal, light it, and burn the charcoal until it is white hot. Once the charcoal is hot, place on top of it a few small blocks or a few handfuls of mesquite shavings that have been soaked in water for about 20 minutes. Fill the water pan and place it above the coals.

Put either whole or halved jalapeños on the racks and cover the cooker. Smoke the jalapeños for about 2 hours. You know when the smoker is cooking properly when the temperature gauge indicates that you are in the ideal range. (The temperature in a smoker will never go above the boiling point of water unless the water boils away. It stays at that temperature for at least four hours and then slowly smokes cooler as the coals die down.)

Once they are smoked, remove the chipotles from the smoker.

To complete the drying process, place the chipotles in a dehydrator or an oven set at 200°F and dry them for 6 to 8 hours. When properly dry, the chipotles should feel light and sound hollow. Store the fully dried chipotles in an airtight container.

Smoky Chipotle Butter

This fabulous butter gives an earthy flavor to mashed potatoes and is also great on fish or beef and on grilled mushrooms and zucchini. The butter will keep in the refrigerator for up to a week and in the freezer (tightly wrapped) for two months.

    3 chipotle peppers
    1/4 pound (1 stick) unsalted butter,
        room temperature

Cut chipotles open lengthwise and remove the seeds and stems. In a small saucepan, bring 1/2 cup water to a boil,

add the chipotles, and simmer for 10 minutes. With a slotted spoon, remove the peppers from the water. Place them on a board, and with a sharp knife, mince the peppers until they make a paste.

With a fork, blend the paste into the butter. This can also be done with a blender or food processor, in which case there is no need to mince the peppers first. Wrap tightly before refrigerating or freezing to prevent the butter from picking up odors.

Makes 1/2 cup.

Spicy Chipotle Almonds

This is a hot little snack, great for a tailgate party. These almonds are terrific with a cold beer. They also give a nice crunch when chopped and sprinkled over a salad.

    2 cups whole blanched almonds
    1 teaspoon canola oil
    1 teaspoon chipotle powder
    1/2 teaspoon ground cumin

Preheat the oven to 325°F. Spread the almonds on a baking sheet. Sprinkle them with the oil and mix them until they are evenly coated with the oil. Put them in the oven and toast them for about 15 minutes, stirring frequently, or until they are lightly golden.

In a small bowl, combine the salt, chipotle powder, and ground cumin. Sprinkle the mixture onto the hot almonds and return them to the oven for 1 more minute. Don't leave them in any longer or the chipotle powder will develop a burned taste.

Makes 2 cups.

How to Make Chili Powders

Chili powders and paprikas are made by grinding up dried, fully-ripe, thin-walled peppers (see page 27 for more information on drying peppers). To grind properly without clumping, the peppers must be brittle and dry. Soggy peppers are caused by very humid weather or if they are frozen. If you need to crisp the peppers, dry them in a 200°F oven or dehydrator for an hour.

You can use a mortar and pestle to grind peppers, but it is easiest in a spice grinder. I find a coffee grinder I reserve for spices works very well for this purpose. First, estimate the amount of dried peppers you need for your recipe. Then, place them in the grinder, and grind the pieces until they are a powder and no large pieces remain. If the peppers are very hot you might want to wear a mask.

Paprika Breadsticks

Any recipe for breadsticks or cheese straws can be augmented with paprika. The easiest way to make it for a party is to use the premade dough sold in the refrigerator section of the grocery store.

> 1 11-ounce package of refrigerated breadstick dough
>
> About 3 tablespoons freshly ground paprika

Preheat the oven to 375°F. Prepare the breadsticks according to the directions on the package. Sprinkle each breadstick with about ¹/₂ teaspoon paprika.

Bake for about 12 minutes, or until the breadsticks are golden brown. Watch the breadsticks carefully or the paprika will burn.

Makes eight 12-inch bread sticks.

Mellow-Yellow Mayonnaise

This is a variation on Carole Saville's recipe for faux mayonnaise—so named because it has no egg yolks. Use your own yellow paprika to add both color and a lovely pepper flavor to the mayonnaise. (You can use red or green paprika as well.) Use this yummy spread over grilled fish, chicken, mushrooms, or eggplant, in turkey sandwiches, and as a dip for artichokes and asparagus.

> 1 large egg white
>
> 2 tablespoons fresh lemon juice
>
> 1 to 1 ¹/₂ tablespoons yellow paprika (or red paprika)
>
> 2 teaspoons Dijon mustard
>
> 1 cup canola oil
>
> Salt to taste

In a small jar with a lid, shake together the egg white, lemon juice,

73

and paprika. Place the mixture in a food processor fitted with a metal blade. Add the mustard. Blend the ingredients for a few seconds, and then start adding the oil in a thin stream, processing until the mixture has thickened. Add the salt and process again for several seconds. Spoon the mayonnaise into a sterilized jar and cover tightly. Store in the refrigerator for up to two weeks.

Makes 1 cup.

Tex-Mex Hot Barbecue Rub

A blend from a spicy part of the world, this is great rubbed on beef, chicken, or pork before barbecuing. In some parts of the American South and Southwest, a dry and crisp coating is preferred on barbecued meat rather than a "saucy" presentation. This recipe is for a dry barbecue and is for the "hotheads." If you don't like your food blazing, substitute a serrano or similar milder chili for the super-hot chiltepíns or see the recipe for Babyback Ribs with Ancho Chilies on page 88.

    2 tablespoons crumbled dried
        Mexican oregano
    1 tablespoon cumin seeds, toasted
    1 teaspoon dried ground chiltepíns
        pequin or a milder chili
    1 teaspoon chili powder
    2 teaspoons salt
    2 tablespoons dark brown sugar

Put all the ingredients in a spice grinder (or use a mortar and pestle) and grind to a powder. Rub the mix on pork ribs, chicken, or on a tri-tip steak

at least 6 hours before cooking, for the flavors to penetrate.

Wrap the meat in plastic wrap and refrigerate it until you are ready to cook. Grill the meat until done to your liking.

Makes about $1/3$ cup, or enough to coat 8 pounds of pork babyback ribs.

Blazo Vinegar

This potent vinegar can be used just like a hot sauce to add flavor to a recipe. The vinegar can be stored in any type of glass bottle, but if you arrange the peppers and spices in a dramatic bottle you will have a wonderful reminder of summer's bounty. Stored on a kitchen shelf, it will give the room "that designer touch." If you can bear to part with it, this vinegar makes a lovely gift.

Remember to choose a container with a neck large enough to fit the largest pepper in your assortment. When choosing peppers, it is fun to mix different colors, but a bottle with all red or all yellow peppers is very lovely too. Let your imagination and your pepper harvest guide you. (By the way, purple peppers turn white.) Obviously the hotter the peppers you choose for your vinegar, the hotter the final product.

To give a rounded flavor to the vinegar, add a few herbs and spices. Choose from bay leaves, cloves, coriander seeds, black peppercorns, star anise, sprigs of thyme, sprigs of rosemary, and a few cloves of garlic. The vinegar will keep for a year and doesn't need to be refrigerated.

    1 quart bottle with a cork or
        screw top
    White wine vinegar, enough to fill
        the bottle
    24 to 36 fairly small hot and sweet
        peppers

If the peppers are not really small, cut a slit in the side or poke them in a few places with a toothpick so the vinegar penetrates the middle of the peppers. Fill the bottle with the peppers and add your choice of spices and herbs. The bottle should be packed fairly full because the peppers will float to the top. Fill the bottle to the rim with vinegar. Cover and set the vinegar aside for a few days to allow the flavors to meld before using it.

Makes about 1 quart.

Salsa Fresca

Zesty sauces and relishes with chili peppers as a key ingredient are the primary condiments used in Mexican cuisine. Here is a classic chopped uncooked salsa to serve with tacos and burritos. This salsa is best used promptly, but leftover salsa can be refrigerated for about 5 days.

    2 to 4 fresh serrano or jalapeño
        chilies (or use milder varieties
        or a combination)
    1/2 medium white onion, minced
    2 garlic cloves, pressed or minced
    4 large ripe tomatoes, seeded and
        minced
    3 tablespoons fresh minced cilantro
    Salt to taste

Stem peppers (seed, too, if you desire a milder salsa) and then mince. Combine the peppers with the remaining ingredients and serve in a small bowl so diners can serve themselves.

Makes 3 cups.

Salsa Cruda

This is the smoky intense salsa Doug Kaufmann made using mulato chilis at his chili tasting. The same recipe also works for mulatos, and dried California and New Mexico peppers. This is a traditional Mexican salsa and is enjoyed on either corn or flour tortillas.

    2 mulato chilis
    2 cloves garlic, peeled

Cut the peppers in two. Remove the seeds and veins if you want a mild salsa. In a dry cast-iron skillet or comal, toast the dry chilis over medium heat. Turn the peppers often to avoid burning them. When they start to get very aromatic, about 1 minute, take them of the heat and put them in a small bowl. Cover the chilis with boiling water and let them sit for 20 minutes. Remove them from the water

and place them in a blender or small bowl of a food processor. (Use a traditional moljete if you have one.) Add the garlic and 1/4 cup of the soaking water and blend for a minute on low speed. Scrape the chili mixture down and blend a little more until the chilis have been ground up. The consistency should be a little runnier than applesauce so add a little more water if needed.

Makes approximately 1/3 cup.

i n t e r v i e w

Doug Kaufman

A number of years ago, I enjoyed a visit to the diverse chili garden of Doug Kaufmann, then a chef in Davis, California. Doug became enamored of chilies during summers spent in Mexico and over the years has become expert in showcasing both the obvious and subtle differences in chilies by giving an occasional chili tasting. Aware that I was trying to learn as much as I could about peppers, he invited me and a few of my friends to his house to sample chilies and identify the differences.

When I arrived, I expected all the chilies to be featured in a salsa cruda (uncooked salsa with fresh tomatoes) as I had experienced before in other pepper tastings. Since the flavors of chili varieties are diverse, however, Doug likes to prepare each one in the way he thinks features its flavors best. Therefore, for the tasting he made a range of dishes in which he served some peppers fresh, either raw or roasted, and featured a few varieties in their dried form.

We gathered in the kitchen to watch Doug prepare his peppers. First, he toasted a few mulatos (dried poblano types) on a hot cast-iron comal (flat Mexican griddle). Soon the air was filled with a heady chili perfume. He removed them from the heat and put them in a small bowl, covered them with a bit of boiling water, and set them aside. He then proceeded to roast fresh poblanos and pimiento peppers by holding them directly over the gas burner until they were charred, then peeled them. For directions on roasting fresh peppers and Doug's recipe for salsa made from dried mulato peppers, see pages 68 and 75. Doug then made a tomato salsa with fresh jalapeños, another with dried serranos, and one with garlic and the reconstituted mulatos. He cut up the roasted poblanos

and pimientos and put them in a bowl, cut up a few other fresh peppers, and we carried the peppers, along with warm tortillas and some condiments, out to a picnic table. With the setting complete, we started tasting peppers one by one by spreading a teaspoon or so of each pepper on a piece of tortilla. We would then discuss what flavors we tasted and how the hotness affected us. Between each type of pepper, we ate plain yogurt and a piece of banana to refresh our palates. After chilies that were too hot, we doused our mouths with lots of yogurt and half a banana.

We tried the dried mulatos first and decided they have mild heat and a smoky chocolate taste. The chopped fresh small bird peppers we declared extremely and fleetingly hot, with a rich, almost meaty flavor and overtones of soy sauce. We sampled a salsa made with dried serranos and found they were quite hot and that after eating them awhile they developed a somber heavy flavor. When we tried some raw fresh 'Yellow Cayennes,' we found them instantly very hot with a clear chili pepper taste. The roasted poblano strips were surprisingly hot, unusually so, and

the pimientos, of course, had no heat at all. Both these varieties had a rich, meaty, sweet, classic pepper taste and were very aromatic. To this day, these are my favorite peppers. Doug ended the tasting with a habanero paste he had previously marinated in lime juice. Just a little taste was enough to send me to the yogurt. That notorious chili lived up to its blazo reputation. Through the intense heat, though, came a complex mix of slightly sweet, slightly floral, even smoky tastes. That afternoon tasting peppers with a pro changed forever the way I enjoy peppers. It gave me the tools to analyze what I like or dislike about a certain pepper and certainly a much greater appreciation for the many flavors and types of spiciness in the *Capsicum* genus. I hope you too are inspired to have a chili tasting with your garden peppers and help us all spread the appreciation for this most exciting vegetable.

Roasted and peeled poblano and pimiento peppers *(above)*. Ripe chilipiquíns and serranos *(middle)*. Serranos, cascabels, yellow and red cayennes, and aji amarillo *(bottom)* at Doug's tasting.

Pepper Ribbon Cheesecake

This is a spectacular, unusual first course and is also perfectly suited for a buffet. Serve the cheesecake with slices of avocado and have plenty of chopped cilantro available for garnishing.

For the crust:

> 2 cups (9-ounce bag) ground restaurant-style white corn tortilla chips
> $1/2$ cup pine nuts
> 1 tablespoon chili powder
> $1/4$ cup unsalted butter, melted

To make the crust: In a food processor, process the corn chips and pine nuts until they have the consistency of crumbs. Add the chili powder and the melted butter and process for a couple of seconds more. Press the mixture into the bottom and up the sides of a 9-inch-diameter removable-bottom springform pan. Refrigerate the crust while you prepare the filling.

For the filling:

> 1 pound natural cream cheese, at room temperature
> $1/4$ cup heavy cream
> 1 teaspoon cumin seeds, roasted and ground

Heat a small dry skillet on the stove, then add the seeds and roast, shaking occasionally until the aromas are released. Cool and then grind.

> $1/4$ teaspoon coriander seeds, roasted and ground
> 2 eggs, at room temperature

Cherry Pepper Shooters

This fabulous appetizer is a classic Italian dish. It can be made with either hot or sweet cherry peppers.

> 24 ripe cherry peppers
> 1 $1/4$ cups white or red wine
> $1/3$ pound Monterey Jack cheese, or fine-quality mozzarella, cut in 1-inch cubes
> $1/8$ pound prosciutto, thinly sliced and cut into strips

With a knife, cut off the top of each pepper. Using a melon baller or very small spoon, scoop out the seeds and pepper membranes.

In a saucepan, bring the wine to a boil. Add the peppers in two batches, poaching each batch for 1 minute. Drain the peppers cut side down on a paper towel.

Take a piece of cheese, wrap a tiny strip of prosciutto around it, and stuff it into a pepper. Repeat the process until all the peppers are stuffed. Place them on a platter and serve.

Serves 6.

4 large red bell peppers

1/2 teaspoon salt

1 1/2 teaspoons chipotle powder

Garnish: red pepper slices and
    fresh cilantro

To make the filling: Put the cream cheese into the bowl of a mixer equipped with the flat beater. Add the heavy cream, cumin, and coriander, and beat on medium speed until the ingredients are well combined. Scrape down the sides of the bowl, add the eggs, and beat for about 1 minute or until light and fluffy. To ensure a smooth filling, scrape down the sides once more and beat 1 minute longer.

Roast the peppers according to the instructions in "How to Roast Peppers" on page 68. Remove the skin and seeds and chop the peppers finely. Reserve a few strips for garnish. In a bowl, blend the chopped peppers with the salt and the chipotle powder.

To make the cheesecake: Preheat the oven to 300°F. Remove the prepared crust from the refrigerator. Spread one-half of the cream cheese mixture over the crust. Spoon the red pepper mixture on top of the cheese. Spoon the remaining cream cheese mixture over the peppers, then smooth over.

You will need to bake the cheesecake in a water bath using a baking dish or roasting pan wider but not deeper than the cheesecake pan. Using heavy-duty aluminum foil, wrap the bottom and sides of the springform pan to prevent water from soaking into the cake. Set the wrapped pan into the baking dish. Bring a kettle of water to a boil.

Set the baking dish with the cheesecake on the lower oven rack and carefully pour the boiling water into the dish to a depth of about 1 inch. Slide the rack into the oven, taking care not to slosh water onto the cake. Bake the cheesecake for 1 hour, then turn off the heat and leave the cake in the oven for another hour.

Remove the cake from the oven; cool to room temperature and then chill in the refrigerator for at least 6 hours. To remove the cake from the pan, gently run a knife around the perimeter of the cake, then release the spring, removing the pan side but leaving the pan bottom.

Place the cheesecake on a decorative serving platter and garnish the top with some red pepper slices and fresh cilantro leaves. To slice into neat portions, use a sharp knife rinsed under hot water between each cut.

Serves 12 to 16.

Deep-Fried Squash Blossoms with Chili Cream

This recipe is from Michael Isles, chef-instructor. I worked with Michael when he was the chef at Mudd's Restaurant in San Ramon, California. The following appetizer was a big hit with the patrons. The sauce can be used with other cooked vegetables, and served over grilled fish or poultry.

For the chili cream:

> 8 mild green 'Anaheim' chilies
> 1 red bell pepper
> 2 cups chicken stock
> 1/4 cup heavy cream
> Juice from 1/2 lime
> Salt and pepper

To make the chili cream: Preheat the oven to 375°F. Roast the chilies and the bell pepper for 20 to 25 minutes. Place them in a paper bag to cool. Peel and seed the chilies and set them aside. Separately, peel and seed the bell pepper, dice, and set aside.

In a saucepan, bring the chicken stock to a boil. Add the roasted chilies, and simmer to reduce the liquid by one-quarter, stirring occasionally. Puree the mixture in a blender for about 45 seconds. Add the cream, the diced bell pepper, and lime juice

to the puree. Season with salt and pepper to taste and set the cream aside.

For the squash blossoms:

> 12 squash blossoms
> 4 ounces goat cheese
> 8 ounces natural cream cheese
> 2 ounces pine nuts, chopped (about
>   1/2 cup)
> 2-inch sprig fresh oregano, minced
> 1/8 teaspoon salt
> 1/8 teaspoon freshly ground black
>   pepper
> Flour for dredging
> 1 egg
> 1/2 cup dried breadcrumbs
> Peanut oil for frying
> Garnish: fresh cilantro

To make the squash blossoms: Carefully examine the squash blossoms for critters and rinse out any you find. Remove the stamens because they could be bitter. In a dry cast-iron skillet, toast the pine nuts over medium heat until barely golden, stirring to prevent burning.

In a small bowl, mix the cheeses, pine nuts, oregano, salt, and pepper. Fill a pastry bag with the cheese mixture. One at a time, gently open the flowers and fill them with the cheese, leaving enough petal length to close the flower tightly.

Once all the blossoms are filled and closed, dredge each one lightly in the

flour. In a small bowl, combine the egg with $^1/_4$ cup of water and mix them lightly. Dip the stuffed blossoms in the egg mixture, then drain and roll in enough bread crumbs to coat them evenly, shaking off the excess.

Preheat the oven to 200°F. Using a large frying pan, pour in enough oil to cover the bottom to 2 inches deep. Heat the oil to 375°F on a deep-frying thermometer. Deep-fry the stuffed blossoms a few at a time until they are golden brown. As they are done, drain each for a few minutes on a paper towel, then place them on a plate and put them in the oven to keep warm.

To serve, divide the cream sauce equally between 4 serving plates. Arrange 3 blossoms on each plate, garnish with cilantro, and serve immediately.

Serves 4.

Walnut-Paprika Dip with Vegetables

Carole Saville, author and herb maven, shared this imaginative recipe with me. It's a particularly savory dip to serve with crudités such as alabaster spears of endive, colorful strips of red pepper, and dark green zucchini. The dip may also be thinned to make a sauce to spoon over room-temperature vegetables. Taste the walnuts to ensure quality; they should be sweet and nutty with no bitterness or rancidity.

1 slice rustic (coarse) white bread, crust removed
2 cups excellent-quality walnuts
1 cup chicken stock
1 tablespoon plus 1 teaspoon ground homegrown sweet paprika (or 1 tablespoon excellent-quality imported sweet Hungarian paprika)
1 teaspoon ground coriander seeds
Pinch cayenne pepper
Salt to taste
Fresh lemon juice to taste
Assorted cut vegetables to serve with the dip

Soak the bread in about 4 tablespoons of chicken stock to soften. Put the bread and walnuts in the work bowl of a food processor. Slowly add the remaining chicken stock and process the mixture to a puree. Add the paprika, cayenne, and coriander and blend again. Add the salt and lemon juice and blend till well combined.

With a spatula, scrape the mixture into a serving bowl. Sprinkle a decorative dusting of paprika over the mixture, and garnish with springs of fresh cilantro.

Makes 2 cups.

Watermelon Spicy Salad

This salad is a blend of traditional Thai flavors. The following recipe was inspired by a TV show I saw with Mary Sue Milliken and Susan Feniger. I missed writing down their recipe, so I tried to re-create it. Here is my re-creation.

For the salad:

    1 small head Bibb lettuce
    4 cups watermelon cubes, seeded
        if necessary
    16 to 20 small shrimp, cooked
    1/2 cup chopped roasted salted
        peanuts

For the dressing:

    1/4 cup fresh lime juice
    1/4 cup white grape juice
    1 tablespoon nam pla (Thai fish
        sauce)
    1 tablespoon chopped mint or
        cilantro
    1 or 2 jalapeño peppers, minced
    Garnish: mint or cilantro

To make the salad: Line 4 individual salad plates with the Bibb lettuce leaves. Put 1 cup of the watermelon cubes on each plate. Add the shrimp, and sprinkle the peanuts over the salad. In a small bowl, whisk together the dressing ingredients and distribute evenly over each plate. Garnish with sprigs of fresh mint or cilantro.

    Serves 4.

Fennel Salad with Red Peppers

This is a basic fennel salad to which I have added the bright colors of red peppers and their wonderful depth of flavor.

For the dressing:

    2 tablespoons lemon juice
    2 tablespoons extra virgin olive oil
    2 tablespoons chicken stock
    1 tablespoon honey
    Salt and freshly ground black pep-
        per to taste

For the salad:

    2 medium fennel bulbs, trimmed
        (1 1/2 to 2 pounds)
    2 red bell peppers, thinly sliced
    Garnish: fennel leaves

To make the salad: In a small bowl, combine the lemon juice, olive oil, chicken stock, honey, salt, and pepper and whisk them thoroughly. Set aside.

Wash and, if necessary, remove the tough stringy outer layer of the fennel bulbs. Set aside a few of the light green inner leaves for a garnish. Very thinly slice the fennel on a mandolin or using a sharp knife. (You should have about a quart of wafer-thin slices.) To prevent discoloring, immediately dress the fennel and mix well. Allow to marinate by refrigerating for at least 2 hours before serving.

To serve, drain the fennel slightly, reserving the extra liquid. Place the fennel on a large serving plate, arrange the sliced peppers over the fennel, drizzle with the reserved dressing, and garnish with the fennel leaves.

    Serves 3 to 4.

Cream of Roasted Pimiento Soup

The velvety green cream drizzled on this rosy-red soup makes this perfect for an elegant first course.

1 tablespoon canola oil

1 medium yellow onion, chopped

2 garlic cloves, minced

1 large green poblano or 'Anaheim' pepper, roasted, peeled, and seeded

10 pimiento or other red bell peppers (about 2 1/2 pounds), roasted, peeled, and seeded

2 cups chicken stock or 1 (14-ounce) can of chicken stock

1/4 teaspoon ground cumin

1/4 teaspoon salt or to taste

3/4 cup heavy cream

Pour the oil into a medium-size non-stick frying pan, heat, and add the onions and garlic. Sauté over medium heat until the onions are translucent, about 7 minutes, and reserve.

In a blender, put the poblano pepper and 1 tablespoon of the chicken stock, and puree to a smooth paste. Using a rubber spatula, scrape the paste into a small bowl, add 1 teaspoon of heavy cream, and stir to combine. (If any lumps remain, force the mixture through a fine sieve.) Pour the green pepper mixture into a plastic squeeze bottle or a small bowl and set aside.

Wash the blender, then place the pimiento peppers, the onion mixture, the remaining chicken stock, the cumin, and salt in the blender and puree. (You may have to do this in two batches.) Pour the pimiento mixture into a saucepan and bring it to a simmer. Remove from the heat and stir in the rest of the heavy cream. Reheat the soup if necessary, but do not allow it to boil or it may separate.

To serve, pour the soup into 4 soup bowls, dividing it equally. Using the squeeze bottle, make a pattern of poblano cream on the soups (or drizzle cream from a spoon in a decorative pattern) and serve immediately.

Serves 4 to 6.

2 tablespoons olive oil

Cayenne, salt, and freshly ground
   black pepper

1 6-inch head of cauliflower (about
   1 1/2 pounds)

In a large sauté pan, cook the onions
and peppers in olive oil until very soft,
about 25 minutes. Remove and puree
in a blender or food processor. Stir in a
little water if the mixture is too thick,
add the seasonings, and keep the sauce
warm.

Meanwhile, cut the cauliflower head
into florets. Bring 1 inch of water to a
boil in a steamer. Put florets in a steamer basket and steam for about 6 minutes
or until the cauliflower is just tender.

To serve, pour about 1/3 cup of the
pepper sauce on each of 4 warm plates.
Put 1/4 of the cauliflower on each plate.
Drizzle the rest of the pepper sauce
over each serving of cauliflower.

Serves 4 to 6.

Mashed Potatoes with Chipotle Butter

Cauliflower with Red Pepper Soubise Sauce

Menlo Park, California, has created a
variation made with red peppers. She
says of her recipe, "This pepper
soubise is both delicious and beautiful.
Try it with steamed broccoli too; both
can serve as an elegant appetizer or
side dish."

These potatoes are great to accompany ribs, grilled chicken, or
smoked turkey.

In France, a classic soubise traditionally has onions as the primary ingredient. Here, Jesse Cool, executive chef
and owner of Flea Street Café in

1 cup chopped yellow onions

2 cups chopped roasted sweet red
   peppers

4 pounds russet potatoes

1 teaspoon salt

2 chipotle peppers, seeds and
   stems removed

3 tablespoons Chipotle Butter (see
   recipe on page 72)

1/3 cup heavy cream, heated

Peel and slice the potatoes. Put them in a pot with 2 cups of salted water and bring to a boil. Add the chipotle peppers and simmer for 20 minutes, or until the potatoes are soft. Drain any leftover cooking water. Remove the peppers and mince them. Return them to pan with the potatoes. Mash the potatoes with a masher. Add the chipotle butter and the heated cream and stir until the potatoes are light and fluffy. Serve immediately.

Serves 4.

Peperonata

This is a traditional Italian pepper and tomato stew, similar to the French ratatouille, sans the eggplant. Try adding basil, oregano, and fennel to vary the flavors. Traditionally peperonata is served with grilled meats or over a plain frittata.

It can also be served at room temperature drizzled with a little olive oil as an appetizer with Italian bread, or you can add a few more tomatoes and use it for a sauce over pasta. I've recommended pepper varieties I have used, but basically any Italian or Cubanelle type and all colorful bells work in the recipe.

3 tablespoons extra virgin olive oil

1 onion, chopped

2 garlic cloves, minced

2 Italian Long peppers (one red, one green), cut into strips

2 sweet banana peppers, cut into strips

1 Cubanelle-type pepper, cut into strips

Optional: 1 jalapeño pepper, minced

6 paste tomatoes, peeled, seeded, and chopped

Salt and freshly ground pepper to taste

1/4 cup chopped fresh parsley

In a Dutch oven, heat the olive oil. Add the onions and sauté them over medium heat for 5 minutes or until soft. Add the garlic and pepper strips and cook another 10 minutes, stirring frequently. Add the tomatoes and simmer the stew for about 20 minutes, stirring occasionally, or until most of the liquid has evaporated. Season with salt and pepper and sprinkle with the chopped parsley.

Serves 4 to 6.

Your Choice Stuffed Peppers

When one thinks of stuffed peppers, bell peppers usually come to mind. All large peppers can be used, however, with one caveat: some varieties have tougher skin than others, and diners may have to remove the skins as they eat.

For the peppers:

- 4 large or 6 medium red or yellow sweet peppers
- 6 ears white corn, shucked; or 2 15-ounce cans of white corn
- 1 tablespoon extra virgin olive oil
- 1 cup sliced green onion
- 2 garlic cloves, minced
- 2 cups sliced mushrooms (about $2/3$ pound)
- 1 green bell pepper, diced
- 1 poblano, jalapeño, serrano, or habanero pepper (your choice: how spicy do you want them?)
- 2 teaspoons ground cumin
- 1 $1/2$ tablespoons fresh oregano
- 1 teaspoon salt
- Freshly ground black pepper to taste
- 3 cups grated mozzarella cheese ($1/2$ pound)

Cut an opening into the side of each pepper and clean out the seeds and membranes. Elongated peppers should look like a canoe. Set them aside.

Preheat the oven to 325°F. Cut the kernels off the corn. You should have about 3 cups.

In a large saucepan, heat the olive oil, add the green onion, garlic, mushrooms, and peppers, and sauté for 10 minutes. Add the corn kernels, cumin, salt, and pepper, and cook for another 5 minutes. With a teaspoon, stuff the hollowed peppers. Place them close together in a greased baking dish. Sprinkle them with the mozzarella cheese and bake them for about 45 minutes.

Serves 4 to 6.

Cooking the Dish Chili

The cooked dish, chili, is truly native to the Americas. Its roots trace back to the Aztecs, who, historians note, made stews with meat and chili peppers. Through the ages, the practice of combining spicy peppers with meat migrated northward until it was adopted by different tribes of Native Americans, some of whom pounded the meat and dried it with chili peppers to make a trail jerky, and others of whom made a green-chili stew. The meat-and-chili-pepper jerky, which was usually reconstituted into a cooked dish, was eventually adopted by trail drivers, who spread this hearty meal throughout the Southwest as they drove their cattle to market. Thus was the passion for the dish most Americans call chili dispersed.

Though there is much heated debate as to whether chili should be made with beans, tomatoes, or other vegetables, everyone agrees that one ingredient is essential: chilies. You can't make chili without them.

Broken Arrow Ranch Chili

This recipe for Texas-style chili comes from *The Broken Arrow Ranch Cookbook* by Mike Hughes. Mike and his wife, Elizabeth, made this chili for me at their ranch using venison, which gave it a richer taste than most chili. To do the recipe justice, be sure to use cubed meat or coarsely ground, not regular ground, beef.

    2 tablespoons cooking oil
    3 pounds lean beef chuck or veni-
        son, coarsely ground or cut into
        1 1/2-inch cubes
    1 (12-ounce) can beer (or more as
        needed)
    1 large onion, chopped
    3 garlic cloves, finely chopped

    1 jalapeño pepper, finely chopped
    5 tablespoons chili powder
    4 teaspoons ground cumin seed
    1 tablespoon paprika
    1 teaspoon salt
    1/4 teaspoon black pepper

Use a large, heavy cast-iron or aluminum pot with a tight-fitting lid. Heat the oil and brown the meat in the oil. Add the beer and cook the browned meat, covered, over low heat for about 1 hour. Stir occasionally to prevent sticking.

Drain the juices from the meat into a skillet and sauté the onion, garlic, and jalapeño in the juices. Pour this mixture back into the pot with the meat and add the remaining ingredients. Cook, covered, over low heat for 1 to 1 1/2 hours, adding more beer if needed. The fun of cooking chili is making your own adjustments. Add more chili powder, cumin, or salt to taste.

Serves 8 to 10.

Black Bean and Chicken Chili

This recipe was contributed by Jesse Cool, owner and chef at Flea Street Café in Menlo Park, California. You'll be amazed at all the rich flavors.

    2 cups dry black beans
    2 pounds meaty chicken (breasts
        and/or thighs)
    Salt and pepper
    1/4 cup olive oil
    1 large onion, chopped
    1/2 cup chopped celery
    1/4 cup minced garlic
    3 tablespoons chili powder
    2 tablespoons cumin
    3 tablespoons butter
    1/2 cup currants or raisins
    1/2 cup chopped carrots
    1 1/2 ounces bittersweet chocolate
    Pinch of cinnamon
    1 to 2 fresh hot peppers, seeded
        and minced

Cover the beans generously with water and soak overnight. Add more water if necessary. Bring to a boil and simmer until tender but not mushy, about 2 hours.

Put the chicken in a pot with 3 cups of water and the salt and pepper. Cover and simmer until the chicken is done, about 30 minutes. Remove the chicken from the broth and reserve the broth. Debone and skin the chicken and cut it into bite-size pieces.

Sauté the onion, celery, garlic, and hot pepper in the olive oil until tender. Add the chili powder, cumin, and butter, and sauté for 1 more minute.

Add the currants or raisins, carrots, 2 cups of the reserved chicken broth, chocolate, and cinnamon, along with the beans (drained of any excess cooking liquid) and the hot peppers. Add more broth if necessary. Let mixture cook, covered, on low heat about 45 minutes. Add the chicken, taste for seasoning, and simmer about 30 minutes longer.

Serves 8.

Garden Chili

Making this chili, full of lively fresh flavors and colors, is a festive way to celebrate the late-summer harvest. Be creative and flexible and use the vegetables and herbs your garden offers. For a vegetarian version, omit the meat and double the quantity of beans and garlic. Serve with corn bread and a green salad.

 1/2 pound dry beans (recommended:
    pinto, kidney, or red Mexican;
    about 1 1/4 cups) or 2 to 3 cups
    fresh shelled beans (omit pre-
    cooking)
 1/4 cup extra virgin olive oil
 2 onions, chopped
 1 pound chuck roast or steak, cut
    into 1/2-inch cubes
 4 garlic cloves, minced
 1 or 2 chili peppers, minced
 3 tablespoons chili powder
 2 teaspoons cumin
 2 quarts tomatoes, peeled and
    seeded (about 8 medium
    tomatoes)
 1 or 2 sweet peppers, diced

 2 small or 1 large summer squash
    (recommended: 1 each yellow
    and green zucchini), diced
 3/4 cup fresh corn kernels (cut from
    1 ear)
 1 1/2 tablespoons minced fresh
    oregano
 1/4 cup minced fresh basil or parsley

Cover the dry beans generously with water and soak overnight. Before cooking, add more water if needed to cover beans and simmer 1 1/2 to 2 1/2 hours or until just tender.

In a large kettle, sauté the onions in olive oil until soft. Add the meat, garlic, chili peppers, chili powder, and cumin, and sauté about 4 minutes.

Add the tomatoes, cover the kettle, and simmer about 1 hour, stirring occasionally. Add the remaining vegetables, the herbs, and the cooked dry beans (or fresh shelled beans, if used) and simmer 1/2 hour longer.

Serves 8 to 10.

Babyback Ribs with Ancho Chilies

All types of flavorings, including ground dried cayenne, paprika-types, and mirasol/guajillo chilies as well as ancho chilies, can be used in a dry rub to flavor ribs. Other traditional flavorings include ground oregano and cumin, brown sugar, dry mustard, and garlic. You can create your own formula using your favorite dried hot pepper or try the one given here.

Accompany the ribs with your favorite barbecue sauce, the Mashed Potatoes with Chipotle Butter on page 84, and coleslaw or a salad.

 4 tablespoons ground dried ancho
    chilies
 2 teaspoons salt
 1/4 teaspoon ground cumin
 1 teaspoon brown sugar
 4 to 6 pounds babyback (loin) pork ribs

Blend the ground chilies, salt, cumin, and sugar in a small bowl. Rub the ribs with the mixture, thoroughly covering both sides. Cover the ribs tightly with plastic wrap and refrigerate for 6 to 8 hours or overnight.

Preheat the oven to 300°F. Wrap the ribs in aluminum foil and bake for 1 hour or until tender. Remove from the oven, unwrap, cool, and reserve.

Barbecue the ribs on a gas grill over fairly high heat for about 10 to 15 minutes. Turn them a few times to make sure they cook evenly.

Serves 4.

Classic Gumbo

Gumbo (an African word for okra) starts with a dark roux and is often thickened with okra and/or filé powder, made from the dried leaves of the sassafras tree. Serve with white rice.

For the roux:

1/2 cup canola oil

3/4 cup flour

1 quart chicken stock

For the gumbo:

2 pounds beef brisket (fat trimmed
   off) or 1 frying chicken, cut in
   large pieces

1/4 cup canola oil

1 pound fresh okra, finely sliced

2 large onions, chopped

1 bell pepper, chopped

1 cup chopped celery

3 garlic cloves, minced

2 hot peppers, seeded and minced

2 cups peeled, seeded, and
   chopped tomatoes

2 bay leaves

1 tablespoon minced fresh thyme
   (or 1 teaspoon dried thyme)

1 to 2 pounds raw shrimp, shelled
   and deveined

About 2 pounds assorted seafood
   such as crab, fish, lobster, and
   crayfish (optional)

2 tablespoons filé powder

Salt and freshly ground pepper to
   taste

To make the roux: In a large, heavy pot, combine the oil with the flour. Stirring constantly with a whisk or wooden spoon, cook over medium-high heat until the mixture turns a reddish brown, about 15 minutes. Bring the stock to a boil and add it slowly to the roux while constantly stirring. The mixture should thicken and become smooth.

To make the gumbo: In a large skillet, brown the meat in the oil. Remove the meat and pour out and reserve the oil. Add 2 cups of water to the pan drippings and boil to dissolve. Scrape the drippings from the bottom of the pan and pour into a separate bowl.

Put the reserved oil back in the pan and add the okra, onions, bell pepper, celery, garlic, hot peppers, tomatoes, bay leaves, and thyme. Cook over low heat for about 1/2 hour, then remove the vegetables from the pan and set aside. Return the meat to the pan, add the reserved drippings, cover, and simmer on low heat for 45 minutes or until tender.

To assemble the gumbo: Combine the roux mixture, the vegetables, and the stewed meat in one pot. Bring to a boil, add the shrimp and other seafood (if using), and cook about 5 minutes. Stir in the filé powder and let the gumbo rest 5 minutes to allow the filé to thicken before serving.

Serves 6.

Roasted Pepper Garden Lasagna

This is a rich lasagna filled with great vegetables. All it needs is a loaf of good bread and a *misticanza* (mesclun) salad to create a feast.

For the lasagna:

- 1 pound dried lasagna noodles
- 1 tablespoon extra virgin olive oil

For the filling:

- 1 pound ricotta cheese
- 1 egg
- 3 garlic cloves, minced
- 1 tablespoon chopped fresh oregano
- 1/4 cup chopped fresh basil leaves
- 1/2 teaspoon hot pepper flakes
- 6 pimiento peppers, roasted, peeled, and seeded
- 1 pound fresh spinach, large stems removed

- 2 cups mozzarella cheese, grated
- 1 cup grated parmesan cheese
- 3 1/2 cups marinara sauce

For the béchamel sauce:

- 2 tablespoons butter
- 3 tablespoons flour
- 2 cups milk
- Pinch of freshly grated nutmeg
- Salt and freshly ground black pepper

To cook the lasagna: In a large pot of boiling salted water, cook the lasagna noodles for 9 minutes or until just tender. Drain them and separate them. Brush each lasagna noodle lightly with olive oil so they will not stick together. Set them aside.

To make the filling: In a small bowl, blend the ricotta with the egg, garlic, oregano, basil, hot pepper flakes, and 2 tablespoons of the Parmesan cheese and set aside.

Slice the roasted pimiento into 2-inch-wide strips and set aside.

Wash the spinach. Steam the spinach until wilted, about 1 minute. Squeeze out some of the liquid and set the spinach aside.

To make the béchamel sauce: Melt the butter in a heavy saucepan. Using a wire whisk, stir in the flour. Add the milk a little at a time, while stirring. Simmer over low to medium heat until the sauce thickens, stirring constantly to avoid lumps and burning. Once the sauce thickens, cook it for 1 minute longer. Season the sauce with nutmeg, salt, and pepper.

To assemble the lasagna: Preheat the oven to 350°F. Brush the bottom of a large (14" x 9" x 2") baking dish with the olive oil. Cover the bottom of the dish with a single layer of lasagna noodles. Spread the ricotta mixture over the noodles.

Cover the ricotta with the pepper slices and sprinkle with 1/2 cup mozzarella. Cover with a layer of noodles. Spread the spinach over the noodles and cover with the béchamel sauce and 1/2 cup more of mozzarella. Cover with a last layer of noodles, and sprinkle them with another 1/2 cup of mozzarella.

Pour the marinara sauce over the lasagna. Sprinkle it with the remaining mozzarella and parmesan cheese. Bake the lasagna for 30 to 40 minutes or until the cheese is lightly browned and bubbly. Let the lasagna sit for about 10 minutes so the juices will be absorbed before serving. Cut in serving-size squares.

Serves 6 to 8.

Golden Chicken Curry with Garam Masala

I learned to make "real" curry from my friend Bhadra Fancy who grew up outside Bombay. What a difference! Instead of a generic mix of spices in a tin, you grind your own fresh aromatic spices, including your own hot peppers.

Called *garam masala* in India, the spices in curry vary from region to region, cook to cook, and from season to season.

A vegetarian version is quite wonderful as well. Here, instead of chicken, whole baby eggplants, potatoes, a whole cauliflower cut in florets, and snap beans are simmered with the garam masala. These curries are served over rice with *raita* (a yogurt and mint sauce) and flat breads.

For the masala paste:

- 1 tablespoon whole coriander seeds
- 1 tablespoon whole cumin seeds
- 1/2 teaspoon cardamom seeds (the seeds from about 6 pods)
- 10 black peppercorns
- 1 teaspoon ground cinnamon
- 1/4 teaspoon ground cloves
- 2 teaspoons ground turmeric
- 1 teaspoon ground cayenne pepper
- 2 teaspoons salt
- 2 tablespoons poppy seeds
- 12 whole blanched almonds
- 5 tablespoons unsweetened coconut milk
- 1 cup chopped onions
- 8 garlic cloves

- 1/2-inch piece fresh ginger, peeled and sliced
- 1 or 2 yellow or red fresh jalapeño peppers, seeded
- 1 yellow or red fresh cayenne pepper, seeded

To make the masala paste: In a dry frying pan, toast the coriander, cumin, and cardamom seeds over medium heat until they just begin to perfume the air. Cool and then combine the toasted seeds and the peppercorns and grind them into a powder using a spice grinder or a mortar and pestle. In a food processor or blender, blend the toasted ground spices and the remaining ingredients into a smooth paste. Set the masala paste aside.

For the curry:

- 2 tablespoons vegetable oil
- 1 (3-pound) chicken, skin removed, cut into serving-pieces
- 1 onion, chopped
- 2 yellow bell peppers, cut in 1/2-inch pieces

- 8 Italian paste tomatoes, peeled, seeded, and chopped
- 2 cups whole baby carrots, or large carrots cut in thick coins
- 8 small potatoes, peeled
- 1 tablespoon lemon juice

In a Dutch oven, heat the vegetable oil. Add the chicken pieces and brown them over medium heat for about 20 minutes or until they are a rich golden brown. Remove the chicken from the pan.

Add the onion and bell peppers to the same pan and sauté over medium heat until they are soft, about 5 minutes. Add the chopped tomatoes, the reserved masala paste, and 4 cups of water. Stir and bring the mixture to a simmer. Return the chicken pieces to the pan, add the carrots and potatoes, and simmer covered for about 30 minutes. Stir in the lemon juice. Serve the curry with rice.

Serves 6.

appendix A planting and maintenance

Covered in this section are crop rotation, mulching, composting, installing irrigation and watering systems, weeding, saving seeds, using floating row covers, and cold frames.

Crop Rotation

Rotating crops in an edible garden has been practiced for centuries. The object is to avoid growing members of the same family in the identical spot year after year because plants in the same family are often prone to similar diseases and pests and deplete the same nutrients. For example, peppers should not follow eggplants or tomatoes, as all are Solanaceae family plants and all are prone to fusarium wilt.

Crop rotation is also practiced to help keep the soil nutrient level up. One family, the pea family (legumes), which includes not only peas and beans but also clovers and alfalfa, adds nitrogen to the soil. In contrast, peppers deplete the soil of nitrogen, as do members of the mustard and cucumber families. Because most vegetables deplete the soil, knowledgeable gardeners not only rotate their beds with vegetables from different families, but also include an occasional cover crop of clover or alfalfa and other soil benefactors like buckwheat and vetch. After growing for a few months, these crops are turned under, providing organic matter and many nutrients. Some cover crops (like rye) are grown over the winter to control soil erosion. The seeds of all sorts of cover crops are available from farm suppliers and specialty seed companies. I've only touched on the basics of this subject; for more information, see Shepherd Ogden's *Step by Step Organic Vegetable Gardening* and some of the other basic gardening texts recommended in the Bibliography.

Following is a short list of related vegetables and herbs. It is not meant to be a comprehensive list but rather to give examples of the types of plants in each family.

Apiaceae (parsley or carrot family)—includes carrots, celeriac, celery, chervil, coriander (cilantro), dill, fennel, lovage, parsley, parsnips

Asteraceae (sunflower or daisy family, also called composites)—includes artichokes, calendulas, celtuce, chicories, dandelions, endives, lettuces, marigolds, tarragon

Brassicaceae (mustard or cabbage family)—includes arugula, broccoli, cabbages, cauliflower, collards, cresses, kale, kohlrabi, komatsuna, mizuna, mustards, radishes, turnips

Chenopodiaceae (goosefoot family)—includes beets, chard, orach, spinach

Cucurbitaceae (cucumber or gourd family)—includes cucumbers, gourds, melons, summer squash, winter squash, pumpkins

Fabaceae (pea family, also called legumes)—includes beans, cowpeas, fava beans, lima beans, peanuts, peas, runner beans, soybeans, sugar peas

Lamiaceae (mint family)—includes basil, mints, oregano, rosemary, sages, summer savory, thymes

Liliaceae (lily family)—includes asparagus, chives, garlic, leeks, onions, Oriental chives, shallots

Solanaceae (nightshade family)—includes eggplants, peppers, potatoes, tomatillos, tomatoes

Mulching

Among the many benefits of mulching is the moderation of soil temperatures. A thick organic mulch helps keep pepper roots from getting too hot in hot-summer regions, and a black plastic mulch warms soil in cool regions in preparation for transplanting. Mulching also reduces moisture loss, prevents erosion, controls weeds, and minimizes soil compaction. When the mulch is an organic material, it adds nutrients and organic matter to the soil as it decomposes, making heavy clay more porous and helping sandy soil retain moisture. Organic mulches include finished compost from your compost pile, grass clippings, pine needles, composted sawdust, straw, or one of the many agricultural byproducts like rice hulls or grape pomace.

Mulch using black plastic

Layers of black and white newspaper are often used for mulching peppers in the Southwest and are particularly good at deterring weeds, conserving moisture, and reflecting heat. The sheets of newspaper are anchored by partially covering them with soil. Like many other organic mulches, newspaper can be tilled or dug in at the end of the season. Coarse, woody mulches, such as wood and bark chips or shredded bark, do not work well as mulches in vegetable gardens because they break down slowly and take nitrogen from the soil. However, they do make good mulches for pathways or other areas of a more permanent nature.

In cooler, short-season areas, organic mulches are applied after the soil has warmed. If your pepper yield is low, the mulch may be keeping your soil too cool for peppers. Use black plastic to warm the soil before planting, and consider partially mulching with black plastic through the growing season. Due to its warming abilities, black plastic is not used in hot climates. When you remove the plastic, dispose of it. Black plastic does not decompose, although there are some brands that claim to; it is more likely that they degrade into small pieces rather than decompose. There are various other plastic mulches on the market, called IRT (infrared transmitting) film, that have the heat-transmitting qualities of clear plastic. These IRT plastic mulches can be green or red. They warm soil more quickly than regular black plastic and also discourage weed growth (which clear plastic does not). IRT is available from selected local garden supply stores and mail-order garden suppliers.

Composting

Compost is the humus-rich result of the decomposition of organic matter, such as leaves and garden trimmings. The objective of a composting system is to speed up decomposition and centralize the material so that you can gather it up and spread it where it will do the most good. Compost's benefits include providing nutrients to plants in a slow-release, balanced fashion; helping break up clay soil, aiding sandy soil to retain moisture, and correcting pH problems. On top of that, compost is free, it can be made at home, and it is an excellent way to recycle

A three-bin composting system

our yard and kitchen wastes. Compost can be used as a soil additive or a mulch.

There need be no great mystique about composting. To create the environment needed by the decay-causing microorganisms that do all the work, just include the following four ingredients, mixed well: three or four parts "brown" material high in carbon, such as dry leaves, dry grass, or even shredded black-and-white newspaper; one part "green" material high in nitrogen, such as fresh grass clippings, fresh garden trimmings, barnyard manure, or kitchen trimmings like pea pods and carrot tops; water in moderate amounts, so that the mixture is moist but not soggy; and air to supply oxygen to the microorganisms. Bury the kitchen trimmings within the pile, so as not to attract flies. Cut up any large pieces of material. Exclude weeds that have gone to seed and noxious perennial weeds such as Bermuda grass because they can lead to the growth of those weeds in the garden. Do not add meat, fat, diseased plants of any kind, woody branches, or cat or dog manure. If you are going to be growing a lot of peppers, it is also best not to put potato peelings into your compost, as they may harbor diseases to which peppers are susceptible.

I don't stress myself about the proper proportions of compost materials, as long as I have a fairly good mix of materials from the garden. If the decomposition is too slow, it is usually because the pile has too much

brown material, is too dry, or needs air. If the pile smells, there is too much green material or it is too wet. To speed up decomposition, I often chop or shred the materials before adding them to the pile, and I may turn the pile occasionally to get additional oxygen to all parts. During decomposition, the materials can become quite hot and steamy, which is preferred; however, it is not mandatory that the compost become extremely hot.

You can make compost in a simple pile, in wire or wood bins, or in rather expensive containers. The size should be at least 3 feet high, wide, and deep (3 cubic feet) for the most efficient decomposition and so the pile is easily workable. It can be larger, but too much so and it becomes hard to manage. In a rainy climate, it's a good idea to have a cover for the compost. I like to use three bins. I collect the compost materials in one bin, have a working bin, and when that bin is full, I turn the contents into the last bin, where it finishes its decomposition. I sift the finished compost into empty garbage cans so that its nutrients don't leach into the soil. The empty bin is then ready to fill up again.

Watering and Irrigation Systems

Even gardeners who live in rainy climates may need to do supplemental watering at specific times during the growing season.

93

Therefore, most gardeners need some sort of supplemental watering system and a knowledge of water management.

There is no easy formula for determining the correct amount or frequency of watering. Proper watering takes experience and observation. In addition to the specific watering needs of individual peppers—which in general average to about 1 inch a week—the amount of watering needed depends on soil type, wind conditions, and air temperature. To water properly, it helps to learn how to recognize water-stress symptoms (often a dulling of foliage color as well as the better-known symptoms of drooping leaves and wilting), how much to water (too much is as bad as too little), and how to water. Some general rules are:

1. Water deeply. Except for seedbeds, peppers need infrequent deep watering rather than frequent light sprinkling.

2. To ensure proper absorption, apply water at a rate slow enough to prevent runoff.

3. Try not to use overhead watering systems when the wind is blowing.

4. When possible, water in the morning so that foliage will have time to dry off before nightfall, thus preventing some disease problems. In addition, because of the cooler temperature, less water is lost to evaporation. An exception is that in very hot climates, overhead watering is sometimes used during the day to cool down the plants and soil.

5. Test your watering system occasionally to make sure it is covering the area evenly.

6. Use methods and tools that conserve water. When using a hose, the nozzle or watering wand should allow you to shut off the water while you move from one container or planting bed to another. Soaker hoses, made of either canvas or recycled tires, and other ooze- and drip-irrigation systems apply water slowly and use water more efficiently than overhead systems.

Drip, or the related ooze/trickle, irrigation systems are advisable wherever feasible, and most gardens are well-suited to them. Drip systems deliver water a drop at a time through spaghetti-like emitter tubes or plastic pipe with emitters that drip water right onto the root zone of each plant. Because of the time and effort involved in installing one or two emitters per plant, these systems work best for permanent plantings. The lines require continual maintenance to make sure the individual emitters are not clogged.

Other similar systems, called ooze systems, either deliver water through holes made every 6 or 12 inches along solid flexible tubing or ooze along the entire porous hose. Either of these systems works well for peppers. Neither system is as prone to clogging as are the emitters. The solid type is made of plastic and is often called laser tubing. It is pressure compensated, which means that the flow of water is even throughout the length of the tubing. The high-quality brands have a built-in mechanism to minimize clogging and are made of tubing that will not expand in hot weather and consequently pop off its fittings. (Some of the inexpensive drip-irrigation kits can make you crazy!)

The porous hose types are made from recycled tires and come in two sizes—a standard hose diameter of 1 inch, great for shrubs and trees planted in a row, and ¼-inch tubing that can be snaked around beds of small plants. Neither are pressure compensated, which means that the plants nearest the source of water get more water than those at the end of the line. It also means that they will not work well if there is any slope.

All types of drip emitter and ooze systems are installed after the plants are in the ground and are held in place with ground staples. To install any drip or ooze system, you must also install an antisiphon valve at the water source to prevent dirty garden water from being drawn up into the house's drinking water. Further, a filter is needed to prevent debris from clogging the emitters. To set up the system, 1-inch distribution tubing is connected to the water source and laid out around the perimeter of the garden. Then smaller-diameter drip and ooze lines are connected to it.

As you can see, installing these systems requires some thought and time. You can order these systems from a specialty mail-order garden or irrigation source or visit your local plumbing store. I find the latter to be the best solution for all my irrigation problems. Over the years, I've found that plumbing-supply stores offer professional-quality supplies, usually for less money than the so-called inexpensive kits available in home-supply stores and some nurseries. In addition to quality materials, there are professionals there to help you lay out an irrigation design that is tailored to your garden. Whether you choose an emitter or an ooze system, when you go to buy your tubing, be prepared by bringing a rough drawing of the area to be irrigated—with dimensions, the location of the water source and any slopes, and, if possible, the water pressure at your water source. Let the professionals walk you through the steps and help pick out supplies that best fit your site.

Problems aside, all forms of drip irrigation are more efficient than furrow or standard overhead watering in delivering water to its precise destination and are well worth considering. They deliver water slowly, so it doesn't run off; they also water deeply, which encourages deep rooting. Drip irrigation also eliminates many disease problems, and because so little of the soil surface is moist, there are fewer weeds. Finally, they have the potential to waste a lot less water.

Weeding

Weeding is needed to make sure unwanted plants don't compete with and overpower your peppers. A good small triangular hoe will help you weed a small garden if you start when the weeds are young and easily hoed. If you allow the weeds to get large, a session of hand pulling is needed. Be cautious around pepper plants, as they are shallow rooted. Applying a mulch is a great way to cut down on weeds; however, if you have a big problem with slugs in your garden, the mulch gives them more places to hide. Another means of controlling weeds, especially annual weeds like crabgrass and pigweed, is a new organic pre-emergence herbicide made from corn gluten called Concern Weed Prevention Plus. This gluten meal inhibits the tiny feeder roots of germinating weed seeds, so they wither and die. It does not kill existing weeds. Obviously, if you use it among new pepper seedlings or in seedbeds, it kills them too, so it is only useful in areas away from very young plants.

Saving Pepper Seeds

While peppers are usually self-pollinated, insects sometimes transfer pollen from one type to another. Hot peppers cross-pollinate much more readily than sweet, and they will cross with sweet as well. In this case, the fruits can become as hot as the dominant gene in the hot variety. If you are concerned about cross-pollination, grow only one variety, or cover the plants with row cover fabric to restrict insect activity. In this event, you need to hand pollinate the hot peppers for the best fruit set. Using a small camel-hair brush, pick up some of the pollen from the flower's anthers and transfer it to the stigma on the same plant.

To gather seeds, harvest the fruits when they are just slightly overripe and beginning to look a little withered. Select those peppers that are just past the point when you'd want to eat them but not yet rotting.

To collect the seeds, you can spoon them out or cut the stem end of the pepper off and tap the seeds free. Wear rubber gloves when working with hot peppers, and do not touch your eyes. Dry seeds on paper towels in a warm, dry place for about two weeks. When dry, store for next year in moisture-proof containers such as sealed jars or self-locking plastic bags. Be sure to label the container with the pepper variety and the date of storage. Store them in a cool, dry place. They may be stored in the refrigerator or the freezer. Packets of silica gel or another moisture absorber can help assure that the seeds will stay dry.

Floating Row Covers

Among the most valuable tools to protect vegetables in the garden are floating row covers made of lightweight spunbonded polyester or polypropylene fabric. They are laid directly over the pepper plants, where they "float" in place, though they can also be stretched over hoops. These covers can be used to protect peppers against cold weather or to shade them in extremely hot and sunny climates. If used correctly, row covers are a most effective form of pest control for various beetles and caterpillars, leafhoppers, aphids, and leaf miners.

The most lightweight covers, usually called summer weight or insect barriers because they have little heat buildup, can be used throughout the season for insect control in all but the hottest and coldest climates. They cut down on 10% of the sunlight, which is seldom a problem unless your garden is already partly shady. Heavier versions, sometimes called garden covers under trade names like Reemay and Tufbell, variously cut down from 15% to 50% of the sunlight—which could be a problem for peppers—but they also raise the temperature underneath from 2°F to 7°F, which can help to protect peppers from late spring and early fall frosts to extend the pepper season and boost the heat in cool-summer areas. Another way to raise the temperature is to use two layers of the lightweight covers.

Other advantages to using floating row covers include:

• The stronger ones protect plants from most songbirds, though not from crafty squirrels and blue jays.

• They raise the humidity around plants, a bonus in arid climates but a problem in humid ones.

• They protect young seedlings and pepper pods from sunburn in summer and in high-altitude gardens.

There are a few limitations to consider:

• These covers keep out pollinating bees (which could be a plus if you are saving seed and want to prevent cross-pollination).

• Many of the fabrics last only a year and then start to deteriorate. (I use tattered small pieces to cover containers, in the bottoms of containers to keep out slugs, etc.)

• Row covers use petroleum products and eventually end up in the landfill.

• In very windy areas, the tunnels and floating row covers are apt to be blown away or become shredded.

• The heavyweight versions may cut down on too much light for peppers and are useful only to help raise temperatures when frost threatens.

Rolls of the fabric, from 5 to 10 feet wide and up to 100 feet long, can be purchased from local nurseries or ordered from garden-supply catalogs. As a rule, you have a wider selection of materials and sizes from mail-order sources.

Before you apply your row cover for pest protection, fully prepare the bed and make sure it's free of eggs, larvae, and adult pests. Then install drip irrigation if you are using it, plant your crop, and mulch (if appropriate). There are two ways to lay a row cover: either directly on the plants or stretched over wire hoops. Laying the cover directly on the plants is the easiest to install. However, laying it over hoops has the advantage of being easier to check under, and pepper plants are sensitive to abrasion if the wind whips the cover around, causing the tips of the plants to turn brown. When

you lay the cover directly on the plants, leave some slack so plants have room to grow. For both methods, secure the edges completely with bricks, rocks, old pieces of lumber, bent wire hangers, or **U**-shaped metal pins sold for this purpose.

To avoid pitfalls, it's critical to check under the row covers from time to time. Check soil moisture; the fibers sometimes shed rain and overhead irrigation water. Check as well for weeds; the protective cover aids their growth too. And most important, check for any insect pests that may have been trapped inside.

Cold Frames

Cold frames are a low-tech answer to a greenhouse and can be used to provide light for pepper seedlings while the weather is still cool (but not severely cold) or to harden seedlings off before transplanting. Start your seeds in the house, and move the containers into the cold frame once the seedlings are established.

A cold frame is fundamentally a shallow box with a glass or acrylic lid, called a sash, that has a back wall taller than the front and is heated only by the sun. It can be a permanent structure or a movable one, and made of wood, metal, or cinder blocks.

Cold frames are available from specialty garden-supply houses and include direc-

tions for their instillation, or you can make your own from scratch. In either case, find a location that receives maximum sun in the fall, winter, and spring—up against the house or a sheltering wall is optimum for warmth. Cold frames located near the house are easiest to maintain, too. You also need an area where the soil under the cold frame drains well.

The size of the sash dictates the size of the cold frame, which is then built in multiples of that size; for example, a 4′ x 6′ sash means a 4′ x 6′ or 4′ x 12′ or 4′ x 24′ etc. cold frame. Greenhouse double-wall polycarbonate plastic windows work well, are more shatterproof, and give more insulation than glass. They are available from building-supply houses and mail-order suppliers. Also consider how much room you need for the crops you want, the ease of maintaining the plants, and the size of your propagation flats. Generally, a cold frame is built into the soil 12 inches and sticks up 12 inches above the soil in front and 16 inches in back, with the low side facing south.

Form the frame with cinder blocks, metal, or wood, and make sure the frame is below ground level and secure so that rodents can't come in under it and the wind can't dislodge it. Build a frame for the sash, making sure it fits exactly. Attach the lid along the back wall and provide a prop of sorts to hold the lid off the frame. To con-

trol the temperature, the lid will need to be adjustable, from a few inches to wide open.

To grow heat-loving peppers in a cold frame, you will need a soil-heating cable or rubber propagation mat to provide extra warmth for growth. These are available from garden-supply houses. These heating systems need a thermostat to control the temperature (some systems include one). Day-to-day maintenance involves regulating the temperature and watering and fertilizing the plants when needed.

Keeping the plants warm is one issue, but it's equally important to keep them from overheating. On a sunny spring day, temperatures inside the cold frame will get high. To prevent this on warm days, after the sun is up prop the sash open 2 to 3 inches; as the sun goes down, close it. Propping the sash open during the day can also help guard against the atmosphere becoming too humid for the seedlings; an overly humid atmosphere can bring on damping-off disease.

A cold frame is a good holding area in which to harden off seedlings. Turn off the heating cable and open the lid more each day. The cold frame protects seedlings against critters or an unexpected frost until they have acclimatized to the intense light of the sun and are ready for the garden.

appendix B
pest and
disease
control

This appendix includes information on how to identify and control possible pests and diseases of peppers. No text on pest control, however, would be complete without also including information on beneficial organisms. The following sections help you identify beneficial insects and give you ideas of how to attract them to your garden. A more detailed aid for identifying pest and helpful insects is *Rodale's Color Handbook of Garden Insects*, by Anna Carr. A hand lens is an invaluable and inexpensive tool to help you identify the insects in your garden.

Beneficial Insects

Attracting Beneficial Insects

The first step to increasing the population of beneficial insects in your garden is to reduce your use of pesticides. Most pesticides kill beneficial as well as pest insects, therefore increasing your dependence on pesticides. The next key step is growing a diversity of plants, especially those that produce nectar and pollen. Ornamentals, like species zinnias, marigolds, alyssum, and yarrow, provide many flowers over a long season and are shallow enough for tiny beneficial insects to reach the nectar. A number of herbs are rich nectar sources, including fennel, dill, anise, chervil, oregano, thyme, and parsley. Allowing a few vegetables like broccoli, carrots, and kale, in particular, to go to flower in your garden is helpful because their tiny flowers are just what many of the small beneficial insects need.

Predators and Parasitoids

Insects that feed on other insects are either predators or parasitoids. Predatory insects such as lady beetles hunt and eat aphids or other plant-feeding insects. Parasitoids, on the other hand, are insects that develop in, or on, the bodies, pupae, or eggs of other insects. Most parasitoids are minute wasps or flies whose larvae (young stages) eat other insects from within. Some of the wasps are so small, they can develop within an aphid or an insect egg. Following are a few of the predatory and parasitoid insects helpful in the garden. Their preservation and protection should be a major goal of your pest-control strategy.

Ground beetles and their larvae are all predators. Most adult ground beetles are fairly large black beetles that scurry out from under plants or containers when you disturb them. Their favorite foods are soft-bodied larvae (such as cutworms) and root maggots; some even eat snails and slugs. If supplied with an undisturbed place to live, like your compost area or perennial plantings, ground beetles will be long-lived residents of your garden.

Lacewings are one of the most effective insect predators in the home garden. They are small green or brown gossamer-winged insects in their adult stage. In the larval stage they look like little tan alligators. Called aphid lions, the larvae are fierce predators of aphids, mites, and whiteflies.

Lady beetles (ladybugs) are the best known of the predator insects. Actually, there are about four hundred species of lady beetles in North America alone. They come in a variety of colors and markings in addition to the familiar red with black spots, but they are never green. Lady beetles and their fierce-looking alligator-shaped larvae eat copious amounts of aphids and other small insects.

Spiders are close relatives of insects. There are hundreds of species, and they are some of the most effective predators of a great range of pest insects.

Syrphid flies (also called flowerflies or hover flies) look like small bees hovering over flowers, but they have only two wings. Most have yellow and black stripes on their body. Their larvae are small green maggots that inhabit leaves, eating small sucking insects, such as aphids, and also mites.

Wasps are all either predators or parasitoids. Unfortunately, the few large wasps that sting have given wasps a bad name. Miniwasps are usually parasitoids, and the adult female lays her eggs in such insects as aphids, whitefly larvae, and caterpillars. The developing wasp larvae usually devour the host. Some miniature wasps are available for purchase from insectaries and are especially effective when released in greenhouses.

Pests

Aphids are small, soft-bodied insects that produce many generations in one season. They suck plant juices and exude honeydew. Green peach aphids, which are light green, are common on peppers, especially when you grow them inside. Look for aphid mummies and other natural enemies mentioned above. Mummies are swollen brown or metallic-looking aphids with a wasp parasitoid growing inside. They are valuable, so keep them. To remove aphids, wash the foliage with a stream of water, repeating daily until the aphids are not a problem. When they are growing on indoor plants and in extremely heavy infestations outside, spray the aphids with insecticidal soap or pyrethrum. Even in the house, check for ants, as they may be "farming" the aphids—ants will move aphids around and protect them from other insects so that they can harvest the honeydew. In this case, you will need to control the ants outside, or indoors, with a boric acid bait for sugar ants available from nurseries.

Caterpillars and maggots are the immature stage of different insects. Caterpillars (including loopers and cutworms) are young moths and butterflies, and maggots are the larvae of flies. Most are not a problem in our gardens. For peppers, the tomato hornworm and cutworms are caterpillars that can cause some problems. In addition, loopers may occasionally chew holes in leaves, and armyworms or corn earworms may feed on the pods. Hand picking cater-

pillars is very effective. Natural controls include birds, wasps, and disease. *Bacillus thuringiensis* var. *kurstaki* (Bt) is a bacterial disease that only affects caterpillars, causing them to starve to death if applied when the caterpillars are fairly young. Brands include Bt *kurstaki*, Dipel, and Thuricide. I seldom use Bt, however, as it also kills harmless butterfly and moth larvae.

Cutworms are usually found in the soil and curl up into a ball when disturbed. They often chew through the stems of young seedlings right at the soil line. To protect plants, place cardboard collars or bottomless tin cans around the plant stem; be sure to sink these collars 1 inch into the ground. Bt gives limited control. Trichogramma miniwasps and black ground beetles are among cutworms' natural enemies but are often not present in a new garden.

Maggots of a small yellow fly with brown stripes on the wings lay eggs on peppers at midsummer in eastern gardens, and the maggots burrow into the fruit and eventually cause it to spoil. If they become a problem, grow your peppers under floating row covers.

Flea beetles are minuscule black-and-white-striped beetles hardly big enough to be seen. The grubs feed on roots and lower leaves; the adults chew leaves so that they look shot full of tiny holes. Flea beetles are too small to gather by hand; try a handheld vacuum. Insecticidal soap on the underside of the leaves and *Bacillus thuringiensis* var. *san diego*, a beetle Bt, have both proved effective. Flea beetles and many other beetle species winter over in the soil, so crop rotation and fall cleanup are vital. New evidence indicates that beneficial nematodes are effective in controlling most pest beetles if applied during their soil-dwelling larval stage.

Leaf miners tunnel through leaves, disfiguring them by causing patches of dead tissue where they feed; they do not burrow into the root. Leaf miners are the larvae of a small fly and can be controlled by floating row covers. Some control can be achieved with neem (described on page 99) or by applying beneficial nematodes.

Mites are among the few arachnids (spiders and their kin) that pose a problem for peppers or any garden plant. A symptom of mite damage is stippling on the leaves in the form of tiny white or yellow spots and

sometimes tiny webs. Mites thrive on dusty leaves and warm weather and on plants grown inside. A routine foliage wash or misting helps control them. If  all else fails, use the neem derivative Green Light Fruit, Nut, and Vegetable Spray, or dispose of the plant. Outside, the natural predators of pest mites include predatory mites, mite-eating thrips, and syrphid flies. Avoid broad-spectrum pesticides as they kill off these predators.

Nematodes are microscopic round worms that naturally inhabit the soil in most of the United States, and particularly in the Southeast. Most nematode species are decomposers, living on decaying matter; many others are predatory on other nematodes, insects, or bacteria. Some of the predatory nematodes can be purchased for pest control, as described below. A few nematodes are parasitic, living on plant roots. Of these, some can be quite harmful to peppers, especially root-knot nematodes. These nematodes make it difficult for plants to take up sufficient water and nutrients, causing stunted-looking plants, lowering a plant's resistance to other problems, and causing small swellings or lesions on the roots. Use resistant pepper varieties; rotate peppers with less-susceptible plants, such as cabbage family plants or French marigolds; plant contaminated beds with a blanket of marigolds and interplant your peppers among them; or if all else fails, grow your peppers in containers with sterilized soil. Southern gardeners, especially, should keep their soil high in organic matter, to encourage beneficial fungi and predatory nematodes.

Whiteflies are sometimes a problem in mild-winter areas of the country, as well as in greenhouses nationwide. Whiteflies can be a persistent problem if pepper plants are against a building or a fence, where air circulation is limited. In the garden, Encarsia wasps and other parasitoids usually provide adequate whitefly control. If populations begin to build up, wash the underside of the leaves with water from your hose. Repeat the washing at least 3 days in a row. Using a handheld vacuum early in the day, while the weather is cool and the insects less active, can be effective, as are insecticidal soap sprays.

Wildlife Problems

Birds can be major pests of young pepper seedlings and are attracted to colorful pepper pods, not surprisingly, as peppers first evolved to be attractive to birds for seed dispersal. If birds are a problem in your garden, cover emerging seedlings with bird netting or lightweight row covers firmly anchored to the ground so that birds can't get under them and feast. Bird netting should also be high enough over the seedlings that they do not stick through it. Once young plants are large enough that the birds leave them alone, you can remove the netting. When fruits start to form, again protect the plants with bird netting if birds are a problem.

A fine-weave fencing will help keep rabbits, mice, and neighborhood dogs out of your garden. If gophers or moles are a problem, plant peppers in chicken wire baskets in the ground. Make the wire stick up a foot from the ground so the critters can't reach inside. In severe situations, you might have to line whole beds with chicken wire. Moles won't eat your plants, but they tunnel through the soil looking for grubs and worms and sometimes disturb young plant roots enough to kill them. Gophers usually need to be trapped. Trapping for moles is less successful, but repellents like MoleMed sometimes help. Cats help with rodent problems but seldom provide adequate control and have been known to graze on pepper seedlings. Small, portable electric fences help keep raccoons and woodchucks out of the garden. Small-diameter wire mesh, bent into boxes and anchored with ground staples, protects seedlings from squirrels and chipmunks.

Deer can be a serious problem—they love most vegetables, including peppers. I've tried myriad repellents, but they gave only short-term control. In some areas, deer cause such severe problems that edible plants can't be grown without tall electric or seven- to nine-foot fences and/or an aggressive dog.

Pest and Disease Controls

Beneficial (entomopathogenic) nematodes may be purchased for control of various insects, including cutworms, leaf miners, and many beetle pests. Make sure you are purchasing the nematodes relevant to the pests you have. Apply them, according to the package directions, when the soil is warm and moist. If you have not had rain recently, irrigate before applying the nematodes. Use any prepared product right away because they cannot be stored once you have put them in a container of water. Using a watering can helps give an even application; agitate the water as you pour, to keep the nematodes from settling to the bottom of the container.

Compost tea for combating powdery mildew and possibly other disease-causing fungi can be made by steeping 1 part manure-based compost in 5 parts water. For example, a gallon of well-aged manure-based compost in burlap and steep it in a 5-gallon bucket of water for 10 days to two weeks in a warm place. Strain through cheesecloth. Spray or apply the mixture with a watering can every 3 to 4 days, in the evening if possible, until symptoms disappear. If harvesting soon, wash the peppers well before eating them.

Insecticidal soap sprays are effective against many pest insects, including caterpillars, aphids, mites, and whiteflies. As a rule, I recommend purchasing insecticidal soaps, as they have been carefully formulated to give the most effective control and are less apt to burn your peppers than a soap spray made at home. If you do make your own, use a mild liquid dishwashing soap, not caustic detergents.

Neem-based pesticide and fungicide products, which are derived from the neem tree *(Azadirachta indica)*, have relatively low toxicity to mammals but are effective against a wide range of insects. BioNeem and Azatin are commercial pesticides containing azadirachtin. Green Light Fruit, Nut, and Vegetable Spray contains clarified hydrophobic extract of neem oil and is effective against mites, aphids, and some fungus diseases. Neem products are still fairly new in the United States. They were thought at first to be harmless to beneficial insects, but some studies are now showing that some beneficial parasitoids that feed on neem-treated pest insects are unable to survive to adulthood. Like all pesticides, neem should only be used as a last resort.

Diseases

Plant diseases are potentially far more damaging to your peppers than are insects. There are two types of diseases: those caused by nutrient deficiencies and those caused by pathogens. Though pathogens are the disease agents, many diseases are brought on by stress to the plants. For instance, peppers get root rot when the plants stand too long with "wet feet"—an ideal condition for the disease, but not for pepper roots. Diseases caused by pathogens are difficult to control once they begin. Therefore, most plant-disease control strategies feature prevention rather than cure.

Nutritional Deficiencies

For peppers, it is especially important to maintain sufficient calcium and phosphorus and the right amount of nitrogen. A lack of calcium can cause peppers to have blossom-end rot, as described on page 100. Phosphorus is necessary for good root growth and for flower and fruit development; without it plants tend to grow slowly. To supply it, work rock phosphate or bone meal into the soil around the root zone before the peppers are planted in the beds. Both insufficient nitrogen and too much nitrogen can cause problems for peppers. Like their cousins the tomatoes, if peppers have too much nitrogen they will produce abundant foliage but few fruits, or may even drop fruit. Too much nitrogen can also delay ripening of the fruits you do get and cause them to be watery and have less sugar, so they are not as sweet as they should be. For many plants, including peppers, too much nitrogen also causes leaf edges to die, promotes succulent new growth savored by aphids, and makes plants prone to cold damage and diseases. However, I find that peppers need more nitrogen than tomatoes. The real trick is to reach a good balance in your soil.

Nitrogen deficiency—shown by a pale and slightly yellow cast to the foliage, especially the lower, older leaves—is especially prevalent in sandy soils or those low in organic matter. If this is the case in your garden or if you are preparing raised beds, supplement your beds with compost and an organic nitrogen like fish meal, blood meal, or aged chicken manure. If your existing plants are showing signs of nitrogen deficiency, apply fish emulsion according to the directions on the container for a quick result, and gently dig in a dry organic nitrogen fertilizer for longer-term needs.

The pH of the soil will also affect how well peppers grow. See "Preparing New Garden Beds and Adding Soil Amendments," page 19, for pH recommendations for peppers.

The following are some pepper problems that may be related to nutrient deficiencies:

Premature pod drop could be due to heat stress, lack of sufficient water, or too much nitrogen fertilizer. Take stock of the conditions and adjust accordingly. Flowers and fruits should return once the situation is corrected.

Blossom-end rot is caused by a calcium deficiency. The symptoms are soft brown rotted areas on the blossom end of the pods and yellowing of the leaves. It is often brought on by insufficient or uneven watering, causing calcium to be unavailable to the plant even though it is present in the soil. Correcting the irrigation, so that plants receive an even supply of water, will often correct the blossom-end rot. If the soil is actually deficient in calcium, try adding dolomitic lime to acid soils or gypsum to alkaline soils when preparing beds. Excessive nitrogen fertilizer and damaged roots can also bring on blossom-end rot.

Diseases Caused by Pathogens

For all of the following diseases, it is important to choose resistant varieties whenever possible, practice crop rotation, use healthy seed, add finished compost to the soil to beef up the beneficial soil microbial community and improve drainage, give the plants good air circulation and sufficient sunshine, clean up fall debris, and avoid overhead watering. Remember, too, that plants infected with disease pathogens should always be discarded in the garbage or burned, not composted.

Anthracnose is caused by a fungus (*Colletotrichum* sp.) that is primarily a problem in the eastern United States. Affected plants develop sunken water-soaked dark spots on the pods. The disease spreads readily in wet weather and overwinters in the soil on debris. Solarizing the soil with clear plastic before planting may help. Neem-based Green Light Fruit, Nut, and Vegetable Spray gives some control.

Bacterial spot (*Xanthomonas campestris* pv. *vesicatoria*) can affect both the foliage and the pods of peppers. It causes small yellowish-green spots on the undersides of young leaves, and dark water-soaked spots on older leaves and fruits. The spots on the pods may become rough and scabby, and leaves may turn yellow and drop. This disease is introduced by infected seeds or seedlings and is spread during warm wet weather. Start your own seedlings using disease-free seeds. Discard diseased plants.

Bacterial wilt (*Pseudomonas solanacearum*) causes plants to wilt, then eventually die. It occurs in regions with mild winters, where the soil does not freeze. To diagnose the disease, cut a wilted stem and look for milky sap that forms a thread when the tip of a stick touches it and is drawn away. Discard infected plants. Dig compost into the affected area to encourage beneficial microorganisms.

Damping-off is caused by various species of fungi and oomycetes (organisms similar to fungi) that live near the soil surface and attack young plants in their early seedling stage. It causes them to wilt and fall over just where they emerge from the soil. These organisms thrive under dark, humid conditions, so the disease can often be thwarted by starting seedlings in sterilized seed-starting mix in clean containers; thinning seedlings so that they aren't overcrowded; keeping the seedlings in a bright, well-ventilated place; and allowing the soil surface to dry between waterings. If you have had a problem with damping-off, do not fertilize your seedlings until they have produced true leaves, as excess nitrogen can favor the disease.

Fusarium wilt is caused by a soil-borne fungus (*Fusarium oxysporum*) most prevalent in the warm parts of the country and in poorly drained soil. It causes an overall wilting of the plant, visible as the leaves from the base of the plant upward yellow and die. If your plants have fusarium,

remove the plants and destroy them. Do not replant peppers in the same soil for many years. Or try soil solarization.

Phytophthora blight, also called chili wilt, is caused by an oomycete (*Phytophthora capsici*) that can affect all parts of the pepper plant, causing root rot, fruit rot, or a leaf blight. *P. capsici* thrives in high humidity, at high temperatures, and in excessively wet soil and can spread very rapidly when conditions favor it. All or part of the plant may suddenly wilt and die. Give plants good soil drainage and do not overwater. There is no cure for the root rot once it affects the whole plant. Remove and destroy the plants and correct the drainage problem.

Powdery mildew, which appears as a white powdery dust on leaves, buds, and tender stems, is caused on peppers by a fungus. Make sure the plants have plenty of sun, are not crowded by other vegetation, and are not moisture stressed. Research has shown that applications of compost tea can be effective against powdery mildew. See "Compost tea," page 99, for directions.

Verticillium wilt is caused by two soil-borne fungi (*Verticillium dahliae* and *V. alboatrum*) that can be a problem in most of North America but especially in regions with cool, moist weather during the growing season. The symptom of this disease is a sudden wilting of one part or all of the plant, then leaves dropping and the eventual death of the plant. If you continually lose peppers, tomatoes, or eggplants, this could be the problem. A cut stem will show vascular discoloring. There is no cure for verticillium wilt and no resistant pepper varieties at this time. Soil solarization may help. Try planting peppers in a part of the garden where you have not grown Solanaceae family plants, or plant them in containers with sterile potting soil. Discard infected plants.

Virus symptoms include stunted growth and deformed or mottled leaves. The mosaic viruses destroy chlorophyll in the leaves, causing them to become yellow and blotched in a mosaic pattern. Tobacco mosaic virus (TMV) can be spread to peppers by hands or tools that have touched an infected plant and by the hands of smokers. Never use tobacco of any kind in the garden. Tobacco users should stay away from peppers and other plants susceptible to TMV or should wash their hands well with soap and water before touching plants. If you have handled plants with TMV, avoid touching other plants and change your clothes and wash your hands and tools well before working with other plants. Believe it or not, milk has been shown to neutralize TMV, so you might also dip your hands and tools in milk. Fortunately, there are many TMV-resistant pepper varieties.

Viral diseases can also be transmitted by aphids and leafhoppers or by seeds, so seed savers need to be extra careful to learn the symptoms. There is no cure for viral conditions, so the affected plants must be destroyed. Do not replant susceptible plants in the same area.

Soil Solarization

A variety of soil-borne fungi, nematodes, and weeds can be controlled by a plastic mulch technique called soil solarization, which uses heat to sterilize the soil. If you have problems with any of the serious soil-borne plant diseases, such as verticillium or fusarium wilt, or if you have a serious nematode infestation, soil solarization is appropriate. (A significant reduction in weed growth can also be expected.) This technique should not be used frivolously, however, because it is a nonspecific treatment, and a good many beneficial life forms are killed along with the pathogens.

The steps of soil solarization are outlined below. The complete process takes four to six weeks during the warmest season of the year.

1. Obtain sufficient clear polyethylene plastic film (4-mil thickness) to cover the treatment area. One layer works well and is usually left on four to six weeks. A double layer retains more heat and halves the treatment time.

2. Irrigate the plot one week before laying down the plastic tarp.

3. After one week, cultivate and level the treatment area. Install drip emitters, soaker hoses, or ditches on 3-foot centers for irrigation during treatment.

4. Place plastic film tightly over treatment area. Do not leave air spaces. Weight edges of plastic with soil.

5. Thoroughly irrigate area under the plastic once a week.

6. One month later, or six weeks if the weather has not been very warm, remove the plastic and plant as desired. It may be left on longer if desired. The longer the plastic is on the soil, the deeper the heat will penetrate.

resources

Sources for Pepper Seeds and Plants

Abundant Life Seed Foundation
P.O. Box 772
Port Townsend, WA 98368
Non-profit organization. Membership:
$30.00; limited income: $20.00
Catalog: $2.00 for nonmembers
Specializes in open-pollinated, heirloom, and endangered seeds

W. Atlee Burpee & Company
Warminster, PA 18974
Carries a wide variety of vegetables, herbs, and flowers

The Cook's Garden
P.O. Box 535
Londonderry, VT 05148
Carefully selected offering of vegetables, including some very nice peppers

Enchanted Seeds
P.O. Box 6087
Las Cruces, NM 88006
Ph. (505) 523-6058
Extensive selection of peppers, including exotic and ornamental varieties and many ideal for southwestern gardens

Evergreen Y. H. Enterprises
P.O. Box 17538
Anaheim, CA 92817
Catalog: $2.00 USA; $2.50 Canada
Asian vegetables and herbs, including peppers

Fox Hollow Seeds
P.O. Box 148
McGrann, PA 16236
Catalog: $1.00
Heirloom herbs, vegetables, flowers

High Altitude Gardens
P.O. Box 1048
Hailey, ID 83333
Ph. (208) 788-4363
Open-pollinated seeds for short cold seasons and high altitudes

Horticultural Enterprises
P.O. Box 810082
Dallas, TX 75381-0082
Specializes in peppers. Ships only to USA.

J. L. Hudson, Seedsman
Star Route 2, Box 337
La Honda, CA 94020
For catalog: P.O. Box 1058, Redwood City, CA 94064
Open-pollinated heirlooms, unusual varieties

Johnny's Selected Seeds
Foss Hill Road
Albion, ME 04910-9731
Excellent selection of vegetables, including many peppers that do well in the Northeast

Native Seeds/SEARCH
526 North 4th Avenue
Tucson, AZ 85705
Ph. (520) 622-5561
Fax (520) 622-5591
<http://desert.net/seeds/home.htm>
Membership: $20.00; low income/student: $12.00
Catalog: $1.00 for nonmembers
Nonprofit organization dedicated to preservation of traditional crops, seeds, and farming methods of the native peoples of the U.S. Southwest and northern Mexico. Membership includes quarterly newsletter and catalog. Offers a very interesting selection of chili peppers, many from New Mexican pueblos and Mexico, plus a good selection of chiltepíns.

Nichols Garden Nursery
1190 North Pacific Highway NE
Albany, OR 97321-4580
Excellent selection of vegetables, including many peppers that do well in the Northwest

Park Seed Company
One Parkton Avenue
Greenwood, SC 29647
Carries a wide variety of vegetables, herbs, and flowers

The Pepper Gal
P.O. Box 23006
Ft. Lauderdale, FL 33307-3006
Catalog: $2.00
Incredibly wide selection of hot, sweet, and ornamental peppers

Plants of the Southwest
Agua Fria, Route 6, Box 11A
Santa Fe, NM 87501
Catalog: $3.50
Open-pollinated seeds of warm-season vegetables, including peppers

Redwood City Seed Company
P.O. Box 361
Redwood City, CA 94064
Ph. (415) 325-7333
Catalog: $1.00 USA, Canada, Mexico; $2.00
other countries
*Specializes in endangered cultivated plants and
unusual vegetable varieties and has a wide
variety of interesting sweet and hot peppers*

Renee's Garden
Look for seed racks in better local retail
outlets. Renee's Garden offers an excellent
selection of colorful, high-quality vegetable
varieties. Call toll-free (888) 880-7228 for
more information.

Santa Barbara Heirloom Nursery
P.O. Box 4235
Santa Barbara, CA 93140-4235
*Certified organically grown heirloom seedlings,
including colorful pepper, eggplant, and
tomato seedlings*

Seed Savers Exchange
3076 North Winn Road
Decorah, IA 52101
Membership: $25.00; low income/senior/student: $20.00; Canadian: $30.00; overseas: $40.00
Catalog free to nonmembers and members
*Nonprofit organization dedicated to saving
vegetable gene-pool diversity. The only source
for many rare and heirloom vegetable seeds.
Members join an extensive network of gardeners saving and exchanging seeds.*

Seeds of Change
P.O. Box 15700
Santa Fe, NM 87506-5700
*Organically grown vegetable and herb seeds,
including some interesting peppers*

Shepherd's Garden Seeds
30 Irene Street
Torrington, CT 06790
*Interesting selection of peppers, many varieties
of European vegetables, herbs, and flowers*

Southern Exposure Seed Exchange
P.O. Box 170
Earlysville, VA 22936
Catalog: $2.00
*Carries many open-pollinated and heirloom
peppers; specializes in heat-tolerant vegetable
varieties*

Stokes Seeds, Inc.
P.O. Box 548
Buffalo, NY 14240
*Carries an excellent selection of peppers and a
complete line of other vegetables and flowers*

Territorial Seed Company
P.O. Box 157
Cottage Grove, OR 97424
*Excellent selection of vegetables, including
many peppers that do well in the Northwest*

Tomato Growers Supply Company
P.O. Box 2237
Fort Meyers, FL 33902
*Extensive selection of all types and colors of
tomatoes and peppers*

Totally Tomatoes
P.O. Box 1626
Augusta, GA 30903
*Extensive selection of all types and colors of
tomatoes and peppers*

Gardening and Cooking Supplies

Gardener's Supply Company
128 Intervale Road
Burlington, VT 05401
*Gardening tools and supplies; particularly good
selection of floating row covers*

Native Seeds/SEARCH
526 North 4th Avenue
Tucson, AZ 85705
Ph. (520) 622-5561
Fax (520) 622-5591
<http://desert.net/seeds/home.htm>
Membership: 20.00; low income/
student: $12.00
Catalog: $1.00 for nonmembers
*Fascinating selection of foodstuffs for cooking,
including red and blue corn meals, beans,
many chili products, and traditional
Southwestern herbs*

The Natural Gardening Company
217 San Anselmo Avenue
San Anselmo, CA 94960
Gardening supplies, organic fertilizers, beneficial nematodes

Nutrite Inc.
P.O. Box 160
Elmira, Ontario
Canada N3B 2Z6
Ph. (519) 669-5401
Canadian source of gardening supplies

Peaceful Valley Farm Supply
P.O. Box 2209
Grass Valley, CA 95945
*Gardening supplies, organic fertilizers, seeds
for cover crops*

Sur La Table
Catalog Division
1765 Sixth Avenue South
Seattle, WA 98134
Cooking equipment

The Urban Farmer Store
2833 Vincente Street
San Francisco, CA 94116
Irrigation equipment

Williams-Sonoma
Mail Order Department
P.O. Box 7456
San Francisco, CA 94120-7456
Cooking equipment

Wycliffe Gardens
P.O. Box 430
Kimberly, British Columbia
Canada BC V1A 2Y9
Ph. (250) 489-4717
Canadian source of gardening supplies

Bibiliography
Books

Andrews, Jean. *Peppers: The Domesticated Capsicums*, New Edition. Austin: University of Texas Press, 1995.

Bender, Steve, editor. *Southern Living Garden Book*. Birmingham, Ala.: Oxmoor House, 1998.

Bayless, Rick with Deann Groen Bayless. *Authentic Mexican: Regional Cooking from the Heart of Mexico*. New York: William Morrow and Company, Inc., 1987.

Brennan, Jennifer. *The Original Thai Cookbook*. New York: The Berkley Publishing Group, 1981.

Bubel, Nancy. *The New Seed-Starters Handbook*. Emmaus, Pa.: Rodale Press, 1988.

Carr, Anna. *Rodale's Color Handbook of Garden Insects*. Emmaus, Pa.: Rodale Press, 1979.

Cathey, H. Marc. *Heat-Zone Gardening. How to Choose Plants that Thrive in Your Region's Warmest Weather*. Alexandra, Va.: Time-Life Custom Publishing, 1998.

Editors of Sunset Books and Sunset magazine. *Sunset National Garden Book*. Menlo Park, Calif.: Sunset Books, 1997.

Editors of Sunset Books and Sunset magazine. *Sunset Western Garden Book*. Menlo Park, Calif.: Sunset Publishing Corporation, 1995.

Faccaiola, Stephen. Cornucopia II: A Source Book for Edible Plants. Vista, Calif.: Kampong Publications, 1998.

Ciletti, Barbara. *The Pepper Harvest Cookbook*. Newtown, Conn.: Tauton Press, 1997.

Cutler, Karan Davis. *Burpee: The Complete Vegetable and Herb Gardener: A Guide to Growing Your Garden Organically*. New York: Macmillan Incorporated, 1997.

DeWitt, Dave, and Paul W. Bosland. *How to Grow Peppers, The Pepper Garden: From the Sweetest Bells to the Hottest Habañeros*. Berkeley: Ten Speed Press, 1993.

DeWitt, Dave, and Paul W. Bosland. *Peppers of the World: An Identification Guide*. Berkeley: Ten Speed Press, 1996.

DeWitt, Dave, and Nancy Gerlach. *The Chili Pepper Book*. Boston: Little, Brown and Company, 1990.

Dille, Carolyn, and Susan Belsinger. *New Southwestern Cooking*. New York: Macmillian Publishing Company, 1985.

Gilkeson, Linda, Pam Peirce, and Miranda Smith. *Rodale's Pest & Disease Problem Solver: A Chemical-Free Guide to Keeping Your Garden Healthy*. Emmaus, Pa.: Rodale Press, 1996.

Hazen-Hammond, Susan, and Eduardo Fuss. *Chili Pepper Fever: Mine's Hotter Than Yours*. Stillwater, Minn.: Voyageur Press, Inc., 1993.

Hughes, Mike. *The Broken Arrow Ranch Cookbook*. Austin: University of Texas Press, 1985.

Kennedy, Diana. *The Cuisines of Mexico*. New York: Harper & Row, Publishers, 1986.

McGee, Harold. *On Food and Cooking: The Science and Lore of the Kitchen*. New York: Charles Scribner's Sons, 1996.

Miller, Mark with John Harrisson. *The Chili Book*. Berkeley. Ten Speed Press, 1991.

Miller, Mark, Mark Kiffin and Suzy Dayton with John Harrisson. *Mark Miller's Indian Market Cookbook*. Berkeley: Ten Speed Press, 1995.

Milliken, Mary Sue and Susan Feniger with Helene Siegel. *Cooking with Two Hot Tamales. New York:* William Moore and Company, Inc., 1997.

Ogden, Shepherd. *Step by Step Organic Vegetable Gardening: The Gardening Classic Revised and Updated*. New York: HarperCollins, 1992.

Olkowski, William, Sheila Daar, and Helga Olkowski. *The Gardener's Guide to Common-Sense Pest Control*. Newtown, Conn.: Taunton Press, 1995.

Peirce, Pam. *Golden Gate Gardening: A Complete Guide to Year-round Food Gardening in the San Francisco Bay Area and Coastal California*. Seattle: Sasquatch Books, 1998.

Pleasant, Barbara. *The Gardener's Bug Book: Earth-Safe Insect Control*. Pownal, Vt.: Storey Communications, Inc., 1994.

Pleasant, Barbara. *The Gardener's Guide to Plant Diseases: Earth-Safe Remedies*. Pownal, Vt.: Storey Communications, Inc., 1995.

Reilly, Ann. *Park's Success with Seeds*. Greenwood, S.C.: Geo. W. Park Seed Co., 1978.

Shepherd, Renee. *Recipes from a Kitchen Garden*. Felton, Calif.: Shepherd's Garden Publishing, 1987.

Shepherd, Renee, and Fran Raboff. *Recipes from a Kitchen Garden,* Volume II. Felton, Calif.: Shepherd's Garden Publishing, 1991.

Somos, András. *The Paprika*. Budapest, Hungary: Akadémiai Kiad Publishin

Troetschler, Ruth, Alison Woodworth, Sonja Wilcomer, Janet Hoffmann, Mary Allen. *Rebugging Your Home & Garden: A Step by Step Guide to Modern Pest Control*. Los Altos, Calif.: PTF Press, 1996.

Whealy, Kent, editor. *The Garden Seed Inventory,* 5th edition. Decorah, Iowa.: Seed Savers Exchange, 1999.

Willinger, Faith. *Red, White and Greens*. New York: HarperCollins, 1996.

Magazines

Fine Cooking. The Tauton Press, 63 Main St., P.O. Box 5506, Newtown, CT 06470.

Other Resources

American Horticulture Society. "The Heat Map." 1-800-777-7931, Extension 45. Cost: $15.00.

Chile Pepper Institute
New Mexico State University
Box 30003, Department 3Q
Las Cruces, NM 88003-8003
Phone: 505-646-3028
email: hotchile@nmsu.edu
Web Site: www.nmsu.edu/~hotchile
Membership is $25.00. Includes Quarterly newsletter; recipes and other publications available; membership directory; occasional seed samples. Call or email if have pepper questions.

acknowledgments

My garden is the foundation for my books, photography, and recipes. For nearly twelve months of the year we toil to keep it beautiful and bountiful. Unlike most gardens, as it is a photo studio and trial plot, it must look glorious, be healthy, and produce for the kitchen all year round. To complicate the maintenance, all the beds are changed at least twice a year. Needless to say, it is a large undertaking. For two decades, a quartet of talented organic gardener/cooks have not only given it hundreds of hours of loving attention, but have also been generous with their vast knowledge of plants. Together, we have forged our concept of gardening and cooking, much of which I share with you in this series of garden cookbooks.

I wish to thank Wendy Krupnick for giving the garden such a strong foundation and Joe Queirolo for maintaining it so beautifully for many years. For the last decade, Jody Main and Duncan Minalga have helped me expand my garden horizons. No matter how complex the project, they enthusiastically rise to the occasion. In the kitchen, I am most fortunate to have Gudi Riter, a very talented cook who developed many of her skills in Germany and France. I thank her for the help she provides as we create recipes and present them in all their glory.

I thank Dayna Lane for her steady hand and editorial assistance. In addition to day-to-day compilations, she joins me in our constant search for the most effective organic pest controls, superior vegetable varieties, and the best sources for plants.

Gardeners are by nature most generous. I want to thank Carole Saville who keeps me au courant, helps document pepper varieties as I photograph, and gives input on recipes.

There are many talented seed people who help me amass variety and growing information from all over the county. They include Renee Shepherd of Renee's Garden Seeds, Rose Marie Nichols McGee of Nichol's Garden Nursery, Rob Johnston of Johnny's Selected Seeds, Joel Reiten at Territorial Seed Company, Craig Dremann of Redwood City Seeds, Jeff McCormack, of Southern Exposure Seed Exchange, and Peter P. Kopcinski of Berkop Seeds. I received additional support from Dr. James Baggett at Oregon State University and Dr. Paul Bosland at New Mexico State University. Thanks too to the growers: David and Karen Winsberg at Happy Quail Farms and Jeff Dawson, garden director at Kendall Jackson Winery, who allowed me to photograph their peppers and shared cultural information. Many thanks to Nona Wolfram-Koivula for locating varieties and photographs and to David Cavagnaro, W. Atlee Burpee & Company, Johnny's Selected Seeds, Park Seeds, and Territorial Seed Company for providing needed pepper images.

I would also like to thank my husband, Robert, who gives such quality technical advice and loving support, and Doug Kaufmann, who invited me into his garden to test peppers "up close and personal."

Many people were instrumental in bringing this book project to fruition. They include Jane Whitfield, Linda Gunnarson, and David Humphrey, who were integral to the initial vision, Kathryn Sky-Peck for providing the style and quality of the layout, and Marcy Hawthorne for the lovely drawings. Heartfelt thanks to Eric Oey and to the entire Tuttle-Periplus staff, especially to Deane Norton, Jan Johnson, and Sonia MacNeil, for their help. Finally, I would like to thank my editor Jeanine Caunt for her strong presence, many talents, and dedication to quality.